Ewen and Roughy's

Real Football Quiz Book

Ewen and Roughy's

Real Football Quiz Book

written by Ewen Cameron
with assists from Alan Rough

First published in Great Britain in 2006 by
Birlinn Ltd

West Newington House
10 Newington Road
Edinburgh
EH9 1QS

www.birlinn.co.uk
ISBN 10: 1 84158 492 4
ISBN 13: 978 1 84158 492 8

British Library Cataloguing-in-Publication Data
A catalogue record for this book is available on request
from the British Library

Designed by Creative Link, North Berwick

Printed and bound by Thomson Litho, East Kilbride

Foreword

Ewen: I'm not sure what to write here.

Roughy: Don't ask me. I haven't got a clue.

Ewen: First up, I have to say thank you for buying this book. I've thoroughly enjoyed putting it together. How about you, Roughy?

Roughy: I've enjoyed reading bits of it.

Ewen: That's right. You've done nothing. So, how come your face is on the cover?

Roughy: It's because I'm the star...and I went to three World Cups.

Ewen: Talking of your face, that's some double chin by the way, big man.

Roughy: I agree it's not that flattering but at least I can get rid of that. What about your nose?

Ewen: Well, you know what they say about men with big noses?

Roughy: Aye, they say 'that's a bloody big nose you've got there'.

Ewen: Let's not get into a war of words here. Let's leave that to the Real Football Phone In. I'm just going to tell the readers what to expect from this wonderful Quiz Book.

Roughy: Great. I can't wait.

Ewen: There are 500 questions and 500 answers.

Roughy: Wow! Impressive.

Ewen: There are 11 rounds and most of the questions are on Scottish football.

Roughy: That's amazing!

Ewen: Will you please just shut up for one minute?

Roughy: Aye, ok.

Ewen: Many of the questions are multiple choice...so you and your mates can argue amongst yourselves as to what the answer is before you look it up.

Roughy: That's really interesting.

Ewen: You're beginning to annoy me now. A couple of other things I need to tell you about. This is no ordinary Quiz Book. This is a Quiz Book with a difference.

Roughy: Oh, this is so great! What hidden surprises do you have in store for us?

Ewen: I'm going to throw this computer at you if you don't stop messing about. As I was saying before I was rudely interrupted, this Quiz Book is different from most. I've included nine great stories that revolve around the show.

Roughy: I can't contain myself...I'm that excited I'm going to wee myself.

Ewen: P*** off then and let me finish. There's some colour pictures and we've also included a CD with over an hour of the funniest moments from the Real Football Phone In.

Roughy: Did you just say, colour pictures?

Ewen: Yes!!!!

Roughy: I need air. I think I'm going to faint...

Ewen: I'm going to ignore you now. If you do get stuck on any of the questions you can always call Roughy for help every weeknight between 6 and 8 o'clock on **0845 100 2 101** or on a Saturday between 5 and 6pm.

Roughy: Are you having a laugh? Why don't they call you for help? You wrote the blinking book.

Ewen: That's really all I've got to say, but before I sign off, I'd just like to thank Mark Benstead and Victoria Gordon for all their help.

Roughy: I don't know what you did...but thanks anyway.

Ewen: Don't forget you can catch up on all the latest Real Football Phone In gossip on our website. What's our website address, Roughy?

Roughy: Errrrr...ww.realradio.fm.com...that's not right is it?

Ewen: Nope. Try again. You've only been working at Real Radio for four years.

Roughy: Errrr...how many 'w's' are there at the beginning?

Ewen: Three!

Roughy: Three w's@realradiofm.co.com

Ewen: I'll do it. Check out our Real Football Phone In website at www.realradiofm.com

Roughy: I knew there was a 'com' in there somewhere.

Ewen: I hope you enjoy the book and the CD.

Roughy Questions

1 How old was Alan Rough when he made his first-team debut?

2 How old was he when he got his first Scotland cap?

3 Who was it against?

4 How many caps in total did he win?

5 Roughy won the League Cup with Partick Thistle in which year?

6 Roughy went to three World Cups – in which years?

7 He went on to play for a team in the US – what was their name?

8 How many years did Roughy spend at Easter Road?

9 Who did Roughy support as a boy?

10 Roughy was named Player of the Year in which year?

11 How old was Roughy when he retired?

12 Who was his final cap against?

13 In his 53 appearances for Scotland how many clean sheets did he keep?

(A) 0   (B) 10

(C) 16   (D) 22

14 Which manager took Roughy to Parkhead?

15 Which keeper replaced him at Easter Road?

16 True or False: Roughy had a trial with Liverpool in 1977?

17 How many of Roughy's caps were won whilst at Hibs?

18 Which two players won their first Scotland caps on the same night as Roughy, then went on to be his manager and assistant manager at Hibs?

19 Who was the manager of Partick Thistle when Roughy and the Jags beat Celtic to win the League Cup (he went on to be assistant manager at Parkhead)?

20 When Roughy played in Thistle's 4-1 League Cup win over Celtic, who scored Celtic's goal?

21 Which keeper did Roughy replace when Scotland faced Wales in a World Cup qualifier in Cardiff in 1985?

22 One of Roughy's most memorable games was against Brazil in the Maracana stadium the year before the Argentina World Cup finals. What was the score?

23 Alan finished his career at Ayr United under which manager?

24 In Roughy's last international game, which former SPL manager scored against him?

25 Alan holds a postwar record against England. What is it?

Over the years I've been very critical of Scottish Premier League referees and because of my big mouth, I somehow got roped into refereeing a football match at Barlinnie Prison between Barlinnie Celtic and Barlinnie Rangers. It was an experience I'll never forget.

Roughy organised the whole event and when he made the announcement on the show, I nearly fell off my chair. I really didn't like the sound of it and, to be honest, I very nearly didn't do it. However, I couldn't chicken out because Roughy and the listeners would never allow it.

Former top-flight referees Brian McGinlay and Bobby Tait were drafted in to assess my performance and be my assistants on the day. As you can imagine, the listeners were winding me up all week in the build-up to the big game. I was sent a chastity belt, soap on a rope (Maggie from Glasgow didn't want me bending over and straining my back in the prison showers) and vaseline (I think one listener was worried about me getting dry lips).

My nerves were shot to pieces. I just wanted to get this game out of the way. We all met at Real Radio on a cold, wet, miserable morning and I didn't say too much as we piled on the bus for the short trip along the M8. Real fear began to set in as we approached Barlinnie.

Two prison wardens greeted us at the big steel gates. But before we could go any further they had to 'frisk' us. The wardens called my name first and led me to a dark room where, to my utter shock, one of them pulled out a pair of surgical gloves. I nearly passed out. Then I heard the roar of laughter from outside. Roughy had set me up … good and proper.

After the fun and games (trust me, I wasn't laughing) I was escorted to my changing room by two of the biggest men I've ever seen. They were there 'for your own protection'. The players (inmates) were warming up in the gym next door and the noise coming through the wall was unbelievable. They were taking this very seriously.

Ten minutes before kick-off, a prison physio turned up to give my legs a wee rub. I declined. He insisted. I didn't argue. As he started to massage my thighs his hands were a wee bit too close to my you-know-what and the oil he was using had a funny smell. It turned out he was rubbing lard into my legs, much to the amusement of everyone watching as they were all in on the joke.

I just wanted the floor to open up and swallow me … but there was no turning back. The time had arrived for me to make my refereeing debut. I've never felt a pressure quite like it. I was petrified. When I walked into the gymnasium, I was welcomed by an almighty boo.

Barlinnie Celtic and Barlinnie Rangers lined up behind me (some of them pinched my bum!). A prison warden shouted 'have a good game boys' and opened the doors to the red ash pitch. As I led the teams out, flanked by my assistants McGinlay and Tait, I was greeted by a wall of noise as hundreds of inmates lined the touchline. I don't mind admitting that I nearly pooed myself.

Now, I ain't going to give you a minute-by-minute account of the game … but in brief I gave Barlinnie Rangers a penalty, which was missed. I handed out four yellow cards, two to each team. When I blew the final whistle, Barlinnie Rangers had won the match 2-1 with a last-minute strike.

I took a fair amount of abuse throughout the game but, all in all, the guys were great. We raised nearly £3,000 for charity and the former referees who assessed my performance said that I passed the test with flying colours and got all of the big decisions correct.

So, if the SPL are looking for a referee…you know where to find me.

Scottish Premier League 50

2

1 What was the name of the linesman who controversially awarded Rangers a last-minute penalty against Hearts at Tynecastle in 2005?

2 How many managers did Livingston go through in five SPL seasons between 2001 and 2006? Name them.

3 Who was in charge of Inverness when they first came up into the SPL?

4 Who was manager of St Mirren when they got relegated in 2001?

5 In what year did Terry Butcher become manager of Motherwell?

6 Which team holds the record for the most goals scored in a single SPL season?

7 Who is the youngest player to turn out in the SPL?

8 Who is the oldest player to feature in the SPL?

9 Which team has conceded the most goals in an SPL season?

10 How many managers have Dundee United had since the start of the SPL?

11 Hearts and Hibs played out a thrilling 4-4 draw in the SPL at Tynecastle in January 2003. There were seven different scorers but one Hearts player grabbed two. Who was he?

12 Steven Pressley has been a mainstay of Hearts in their time in the SPL, but which two other SPL sides did he previously play for?

13 Which club was Tony Mowbray with before he took over as manager of Hibs in 2004?

14 Rangers beat Celtic 2-0 in November 2004 and two Hoops players were sent off. Who were they?

15 Which team's mascot caused controversy in 2005 by putting bandages on his knees ahead of a game with Celtic, poking fun at Bobo Balde's reputation for tough tackling?

16 Which two teams scored seven or more goals in single SPL games in 2006?

17 In what year were St Johnstone relegated from the SPL?

18 Which team did Craig Levein leave Hearts for in 2004?

19 How much did Blackburn pay for Barry Ferguson in 2003?

20 Which player holds the record for most SPL hat-tricks, with 12?

21 Why did Motherwell avoid relegation from the SPL in 2003 despite finishing bottom of the table?

22 Which two players share the tag of Martin O'Neill's most expensive signing for Celtic?

23 How much did Arsenal pay Rangers for Giovanni van Bronckhorst in 2001?

24 From which club did Hearts buy midfielder Paul Hartley in 2003?

25 Who holds the record for the lowest-ever SPL points total?

26 Celtic Park is the biggest stadium in the SPL but how many supporters can it hold?

27 Who scored the first-ever SPL goal?

28 In the first SPL campaign in 1998/1999 which team landed a Uefa Cup spot through fair play?

29 Who was the SPL's top goal scorer and SPFA Player of the Year in 1999/2000?

30 In what year did the SPL expand to 12 teams?

31 Which foreign boss took over at Dens Park in 2000?

32 How many SPL goals did Claudio Caniggia score for Dundee?

33 In which position did Livingston finish in their first season in the SPL?

34 Celtic clinched back-to-back league titles in 2001/2002, but how long had it been since they last achieved it?

35 How many league games did Celtic lose during their 2001/2002 campaign?

36 In which SPL season did Rangers clinch a record-breaking 50th league title?

37 Who was named SPFA Young Player of the Year in 2003/2004?

(A) Stephen Pearson   (B) Derek Riordan
(C) Zander Diamond   (D) David Marshall

38 How many seats must a stadium have to meet the SPL standard?

(A) 10,000   (B) 8,000
(C) 7,000   (D) 6,000

39 Who did John Robertson become manager of after leaving Hearts in 2005?

40 Martin O'Neill was a phenomenon at Celtic, but which three clubs had he previously managed?

41 Which two clubs did Alex McLeish manage before Rangers?

42 What is the name of the Serbian midfielder signed by Motherwell in 2000? Earlier in his career Aston Villa paid £4m for him.

43 How many days did Craig Burley spend at Dens Park in his short-lived spell as a Dundee player?

(A) 34   (B) 74

(C) 84   (D) 104

44 Which two players were put in charge of Partick Thistle as the Jags battled against the drop in 2004?

45 From which club did Falkirk sign mercurial midfielder Russell Latapy?

46 How many SPL goals did Henrik Larsson score during his time at Celtic?

(A) 168   (B) 158

(C) 178   (D) 148

47 What was the name of the Brazilian international signed by Rangers in 2003?

48 How many players did Hearts sign in the January 2006 transfer window? (clue – it took a bus to get them all in)

49 Which player scored from the spot for Rangers in the controversial 2-1 win over Hearts at Tynecastle in 2005?

50 Which England international joined Celtic on loan in 2003 but only made two league starts?

I've experienced quite a few embarrassing moments in my three years hosting the Real Football Phone In. But the day I stripped naked to run around Ibrox will be very difficult to beat.

It all began with the rumour that Jean Alain Boumsong was considering a move to Rangers. The French defender's contract with Auxerre was coming to an end and Liverpool, Inter Milan and a few Spanish sides were all reported to be interested in the player. I just couldn't see how Rangers could persuade him to come and play in the SPL. Surely, he'd want to ply his trade in the Premiership or Serie A or La Liga?

Anyway, it was a hotly debated topic on the show and Roughy was convinced that Rangers had a very good chance of signing Boumsong. I laughed. And then I laughed again.
'Roughy, don't be stupid. There's no chance he's coming here. I tell you what, mate, if Rangers win his signature I'll run naked at Ibrox.'

That night, at around 9.30, I got a text message from Keith Jackson at the Daily Record. *'If I were you I'd get myself down to the gym first thing in the morning.'*
I felt sick. This was surely a wind-up. I called Keith.
'Mate, please tell me it's not going to happen.'
'Sorry, Ewen, I have it on good authority that Jean Alain Boumsong will be signing for Rangers.'
'Is the deal done?'
'Not yet. But Rangers are red-hot favourites.'

There was still a glimmer of hope that I wouldn't have to show my bits to the people of Govan. I called a contact in Liverpool to find out if Gerard Houllier was still trying to bring the defender to Anfield.
'Liverpool's interest has cooled because they can't agree on a contract.'
'Who will sign him?'
Please say Inter Milan. Please say Inter Milan.
'I think he will be going to Rangers.'
'NOOOOOOOOOOOOOOOOOOOOOOOOOooooooooooooo…'

I didn't get much sleep that night. And when I did crash out I'd wake up 20 minutes later in a cold sweat. This was a living nightmare.

The following day the tabloid newspapers confirmed that the French international was joining Rangers on a free transfer. I'm sure I don't need to tell you that the listeners and Roughy lapped this one up. The show was taken over by women who wanted to know if I was 'packing a monster' or a 'chipolata sausage'.

Roughy insisted I pick a date for the naked run. I was being backed into a corner. I needed to get out of this. I needed some divine intervention. It arrived in the form of Carol Patton at the Rangers PR department.

'Ewen, our head of security won't let you run naked inside Ibrox.'
'Yes!' I screamed. But the joy was short-lived.
'However, there's nothing to stop you from running naked outside the stadium. I could do with a good laugh.'
I looked to the heavens and said: 'Beam me up, Scotty.' It didn't work. I was going to have to go through with this.

Two weeks later, the day of the run. On a very, very cold December morning. The only good news was that I wasn't allowed to go completely starkers. I would have to wear a tiny g-string to cover up my 'monster'. I headed to Ann Summers and picked up a little red number with Santa on the front saying 'I've got a rather big present for you inside'. As I approached Ibrox I could see plenty press photographers. Could it get any worse?

Roughy was there all wrapped up in his big coat laughing his head off. There were many listeners as well. Mostly women, I might add. And then the Rangers PR department (all women) turned up with a video camera. What were they hoping to see?

I got changed in the back of a people carrier with tinted windows. I put on the g-string, a Rangers Christmas hat and wrapped tinsel around my neck. When I jumped out of the van everyone fell about laughing. I gave a wee wave and started my run past the main stand.

The street was lined with people laughing and clapping. As I approached the main door at Ibrox I noticed the ground staff in their blue overalls. Unbeknownst to me, Roughy had spoken to the guys earlier. Out of the blue (no pun intended) FIVE buckets of freezing cold water were hurled at me. It was like running into a brick wall. I couldn't believe it. But I soldiered on and completed my run.

All pictures from that particular day have been burned, but unfortunately there is a video floating around. If you do come across it, then I suggest you think long and hard before viewing it because it's not for the faint-hearted and could scare the kids.

Celtic Questions

3

1 Celtic recorded their highest-ever attendance in 1938. How many watched the Hoops play Rangers?

(A) 84,000   (B) 88,000

(C) 92,000   (D) 96,000

2 Who did Celtic beat in their first official match in 1888?

(A) Rangers   (B) Hearts

(C) Hibs   (D) Clydebank

3 In which year did Celtic win their first-ever Scottish Cup?

(A) 1889   (B) 1890

(C) 1891   (D) 1892

4 Over 146,000 fans (a record in European club competition) turned up at Hampden Park to watch Celtic win the Scottish Cup in 1937. Who did they beat 2-1?

(A) Aberdeen   (B) Rangers

(C) Hearts   (D) Dundee Utd

5 Who replaced Jimmy McStay as manager in 1945?

6 Celtic thrashed Rangers in the 1957 League Cup final. What was the score?

7 In which year was Jock Stein named Celtic manager?

(A) 1963   (B) 1964

(C) 1965   (D) 1966

8 What was Jock Stein's first trophy as Celtic manager?

(A) Scottish Cup   (B) League Cup

(C) League Championship (D) Coronation Cup

9 Who scored the goals in Celtic's 2-1 victory over Inter Milan in the 1967 European Cup final?

10 Celtic were knocked out of the European Cup at the semi-final stage in 1972. Inter Milan won on penalties. Who missed the opening spot kick for Celtic?

11 In what year did Celtic win their ninth title in a row?

12 How many trophies did Jock Stein deliver during his 12-year tenure as Celtic manager?

(A) 21   (B) 23

(C) 25   (D) 27

13 Who took control of Celtic in 1994 and ousted the board?

14 In what season did Celtic play their home games at Hampden Park?

15 What nationality is former Celtic manager Wim Jansen?

16 Celtic beat Kilmarnock 3-0 in the League Cup final in 2001. Who scored the goals?

17 How many goals did Henrik Larsson score in season 2001/2002?

(A) 51   (B) 53

(C) 55   (D) 57

18 On the way to reaching the Uefa Cup final in 2003, Celtic beat two English clubs. Name the teams and the aggregate scores.

19 How many league goals did Jimmy McGrory score for Celtic between 1922 and 1937?

(A) 397   (B) 401

(C) 405   (D) 409

20 Up to and including season 2005/2006, what is the highest transfer fee paid by Celtic for a player?

21 How much did Celtic pay Feyenoord for Henrik Larsson?

22 Name the SFA Chief Executive who delayed the registration of Jorge Cadete.

23 Who is Celtic's most capped internationalist?

(A) Pat Bonner   (B) Paul McStay

(C) Billy McNeill   (D) Tommy Burns

24 What is Celtic's record victory?

(A) 11-0 v Dundee   (B) 12-0 v Morton

(C) 13-0 v Clydebank   (D) 14-0 v St Mirren

25 Who scored one of the fastest-ever hat-tricks in European club football in 2000?

(A) Mark Burchill   (B) Mark Viduka

(C) Henrik Larsson   (D) Chris Sutton

26 How many league points did Celtic win in season 2001/2002?

(A) 99   (B) 101

(C) 103   (D) 105

27 Celtic currently hold the UK record for the longest unbeaten run in professional football. How many games?

28 Celtic paid £1.5m for defender Adam Virgo in 2005. Where did he sign from?

29 Which two players signed pre-contract agreements with Celtic in January 2006?

30 Celtic's top three all-time scorers are Jimmy McGrory, Bobby Lennox and Henrik Larsson. Who is fourth on the all-time list with 232 goals?

(A) Jimmy Quinn   (B) John Hughes

(C) Sandy McMahon   (D) Stevie Chalmers

31 Who made a record 486 appearances for Celtic?

(A) Paul McStay   (B) Jimmy McGrory

(C) Billy McNeill   (D) Bobby Lennox

32 What shirt number did Craig Beattie wear during season 2005/2006?

33 In what year did Neil Lennon join Celtic?

34 Bertie Auld returned to Celtic from which English club in 1965?

(A) Aston Villa   (B) Birmingham

(C) West Brom   (D) Sunderland

35 Who is the only player in Scottish football history to score hat-tricks in both Scottish Cup and League Cup finals?

36 Which two Celtic players won the SPFA Player of the Year and SPFA Young Player of the Year awards in 1983?

37 In which year was Kenny Dalglish made captain of Celtic?

(A) 1973   (B) 1974

(C) 1975   (D) 1976

38 Celtic sold Kenny Dalglish to Liverpool in 1977 for a then record transfer fee. What was the amount?

(A) £440,000   (B) £460,000

(C) £480,000   (D) £500,000

39 Mo Johnston spent three seasons at Celtic. How many goals did he score in total for the Parkhead side?

(A) 45   (B) 55

(C) 65   (D) 75

40 The European Cup-winning side of 1967 were all born within how many miles of Glasgow?

(A) 25   (B) 30

(C) 35   (D) 40

41 Who did Jackie McNamara play for before signing for Celtic in 1995?

42 Name the three clubs John Hartson played for between Arsenal and Celtic.

43 Who did Celtic beat in Martin O'Neill's final game in charge?

44 Between 2001 and 2004, how many games did Celtic go unbeaten at home?

(A) 71   (B) 74

(C) 77   (D) 80

45 Who did Celtic beat in the semi-finals to reach the 2003 Uefa Cup final?

46 Who did Martin O'Neill replace as Celtic manager?

47 Celtic won every competition they entered in 1967. Name all five.

48 Who beat Celtic 2-1 after extra-time in the 1970 European Cup final?

(A) Feyenoord   (B) Benfica

(C) Bayern Munich   (D) Roma

49 According to Celtic fans, when was the club's most famous song 'You'll Never Walk Alone' first sung?

(A) 1957 – After the 7-1 League Cup victory over Rangers

(B) 1967 – After the 2-1 victory over Inter Milan in the European Cup final

(C) 1974 – After securing their ninth straight Scottish League title

(D) 1985 – After winning the Scottish League title on the final day of the season

50 Who was voted the greatest-ever player by the fans?

Regular listeners to the Real Football Phone In will be aware of the stupid bets Roughy and I make on a regular basis. Unfortunately for me I lose nine times out of ten. I then end up doing something really stupid…like running naked at Ibrox!
However, Mr Rough did lose one bet he has lived to regret.

Cast your mind back to the last time Partick Thistle were in the SPL. Roughy's beloved Jags were certainties to finish bottom. But there was a chance they'd avoid relegation because Inverness Caley Thistle's stadium didn't have the required 10,000 seats for the top flight. Inverness put forward a proposal to ground-share with Aberdeen. Very few expected this to be approved.

'You can't just change the rules just like that,' said Roughy. 'Everyone knew the criteria to get promoted at the start of the season. I feel sorry for Inverness, but rules are rules.'

I disagreed. 'Inverness deserve their place in the SPL and everything should be done to make sure they get there. And if that means ground-sharing with Aberdeen…then great.'

This debate raged for days. The listeners were split down the middle and it was looking more and more likely that Partick would survive. It was at this point I made a bet with Roughy.
'If the Jags are relegated…you have to bring back your famous 1978 perm.'
At first he declined. But the listeners refused to let him get away with it that easily.
'Roughy, if you're so confident Partick won't get relegated…then you have to take up the bet,' said a man from Glasgow.
Through gritted teeth, the big man accepted.

Roughy's hair was now in the hands of the SPL board. Their meeting was only days away. Would they allow Inverness to ground-share with Aberdeen and take their rightful place in the Premier League or would Partick get the vote?

I waited with the media outside Hampden for the outcome. Many of the journalists were talking about Roughy. After two hours of waiting an SPL spokesman emerged and gave us the news which prompted a scream of joy from me. Inverness were being promoted. Partick were heading into the First Division. Roughy was getting his hair permed!

Three months pass and my sidekick thinks I've forgotten about his hair. I call my colleague, Steve McKenna.
'Mate, I need your help. Who could we get to perm Roughy's hair, live on the show?'
Steve came up with the goods…big style.

On the night of the live hair-perm, the hairdresser is hiding in the back office with his assistant. Everyone has been briefed not to say a word. Roughy arrives. Gary MacKay is on the show too as Roughy will be busy getting his hair done. I begin the show.

'Before we take your calls, I have something to say. Three months ago, Mr Rough placed a bet with the nation. He said that if Partick Thistle were relegated then he'd get his hair permed.'

The colour drained from Roughy's face. Gary MacKay started giggling. All the other staff began to gather in the studio next door.
'TONIGHT, ROUGHY, THIS IS YOUR PERM!' I shouted.
The door burst open and in walked Taylor Ferguson, hairdresser to the stars.

Taylor didn't mess about and got to work on Roughy's hair straight away. It's probably the hardest show I've ever done because I couldn't stop laughing. It got so bad we had to send Roughy out of the studio because the sight of him with curlers in his hair was just too much. Gary and I nearly wet ourselves.

It was the 1978 World Cup all over again. And since that day, Roughy hasn't placed another stupid bet!

Ha ha   Ha ha
Ha ha

Me laughing non-stop

Roughy with his 'trendy' perm!

The Premiership

1 Who scored the first-ever Premiership goal?

2 Who scored the 10,000th Premiership goal?

3 How many Premiership titles have Man United won?

4 How many points were Newcastle ahead of Man United at Christmas in the 1995/1996 season before they famously blew their title hopes?

5 Which two strikers share the honour of scoring the most goals in a single Premiership season?

6 How many did they score?

7 Four English players have commanded transfer fees in excess of £7m playing in the Premiership but have never been capped for England. Who are they?

8 Arsenal broke the record for games unbeaten in the English top flight in 2005. How long did their run stretch?

9 Who beat them to end the sequence?

10 Who did Arsene Wenger manage before taking over at Arsenal?

11 Which English team did Eric Cantona first join on trial?

12 Who succeeded Ray Harford as manager of Blackburn Rovers in 1997?

13 How much in total has Rio Ferdinand cost in transfer fees?

14 David Beckham famously scored from within his own half in the Premiership. Against which team?

15 Which former Scotland international was named English football writers' Player of the Year in 1991, over a decade after he was named Scottish football writers' Player of the Year?

16 What's the lowest-ever points tally for a Premiership side? And who got it?

17 Who were the first team to field an all-foreign starting XI?

18 Who scored the first Premiership hat-trick?

19 How many Premiership goals did Celtic striker Dion Dublin score?

(A) 55   (B) 111

(C) 99   (D) 33

20 Who is the tallest player to play in the Premiership?

21 Who is the youngest?

22 Who holds the record for the fastest-ever Premiership hat-trick, bagged in four minutes 32 seconds?

23 Who holds the record for the fewest goals conceded in a season?

24 How many did they let in?

25 Which team has scored the most goals in a single Premiership season?

26 Fewest goals scored by a team in a Premiership season?

27 Most clean sheets in a single Premiership season?

28 Who is the youngest-ever player with a Premiership winners' medal?

29 What is the name of the teen sensation snapped up by Arsenal from Southampton midway through the 2005/2006 season?

30 Which player was put in charge of Crystal Palace during the 1997/1998 season after Steve Coppell was moved upstairs? (His assistant at the time was the Swede Thomas Brolin, which may or may not help you!)

31 Fabrizio Ravanelli spent 13 months with Middlesbrough in the Premiership. In all competitions how many goals did he score?

(A) 31   (B) 33

(C) 35   (D) 37

32 Which team did Spurs sign Jurgen Klinsmann from in 1994?

33 Matt Le Tissier was a bit of a penalty expert for Southampton. What was his record?

(A) 49/50   (B) 65/70

(C) 69/70   (D) 45/50

34 Who holds the record for the most Premiership appearances?

35 Wayne Rooney burst onto the scene for Everton in season 2002/2003. It took him nine games to get his first goal, but when he did, who was it against?

36 The Premiership has been home to some of the world's greatest strikers, but how many of them have won the Golden Boot at a World Cup?

37 How many European trophies have been won by English sides since the Premiership began?

38 Liverpool's 4-3 defeat of Newcastle at Anfield in April 1996 was voted the best-ever Premiership match. Two Liverpool players grabbed braces in the game. Who were they?

39 In April 1995, Man United hammered Ipswich 9-0 at Old Trafford to record the highest-ever Premiership win. Which player helped himself to five goals that day?

40 Who was named PFA Player of the Year for 2004/2005?

41 How many different teams have won the Premiership?

42 Who finished bottom of the table that first Premiership season?

43 Shay Given has played in the Premiership for over a decade, but which team did he initially join in 1993?

44 Which team did David Beckham join on loan to gain experience before breaking into the Man United first team?

45 Which Premiership player was banned for pushing over referee Paul Alcock after being shown the red card?

46 How many games was he banned for?

47 What did Robbie Fowler do after scoring a goal against Everton in 1999 that landed him with a hefty fine from the FA?

48 How many English clubs did Italian striker Benito Carbone play for, and who were they?

49 What was the nickname given to former Chelsea boss Claudio Ranieri?

50 Who captained Man United to their first Premiership title?

And then there were two

The Real Football Phone In team was nominated for a prestigious Sony Radio Academy Award in 2006. It was a great honour to be named as one of the top five sports programmes in the country and we were all extremely proud. It meant flying to London for the gala evening at the Grosvenor House Hotel.

Of course, we wanted to look the part and Roughy and I decided we'd wear kilts. Great idea, you'd think? I certainly did … at the time.

A kilt company offered to dress us for the biggest night of our radio careers. We went to meet them and they'd already decided what we should wear based on our personalities. At first I wasn't sure about my outfit, but as soon as I put it on … I loved it. Put it this way, you would have spotted me in a crowd. As for Roughy, he went for a more traditional look. We didn't have to pay for a thing. Everything was provided, including Skean Dhu.

On the morning of our flight to London, I decided I'd leave the Skean Dhu behind. I really didn't see the point in taking it on the plane, even though it could go through with your luggage. When I arrived at Roughy's house, he was packed and ready to go. We jumped in the car and headed to Glasgow Airport. London, here we come.

Everything was going great. There wasn't much of a queue at check-in. The flight was on time and the sun was shining. The young lady asked us if we had any sharp objects in our luggage.

'Yes,' Roughy replied. 'I've packed my Skean Dhu in my case.'

'Are you sure it's there, sir, and not in your hand luggage?' asked the check-in girl.

'Yes, I'm sure,' said Roughy.

I wasn't convinced and asked him to have a look in his hand luggage. He rummaged around for a few seconds and said 'It's definitely in my case.' The young lady then handed us our boarding passes and wished us a 'happy flight'.

So, we headed to the gate to catch our plane. I was ahead of Roughy in the queue and got through security without a problem. Waiting to board the aircraft, I notice that Roughy was nowhere to be seen.

Our producer, Victoria, then came running towards me. 'Roughy has been stopped by security because they've found a dagger in his hand luggage and they've taken him away,' she says. I just burst out laughing. Victoria and I boarded the plane. I fully expected Roughy to tell the security people to keep the Skean Dhu and join us.

How wrong I was. To our horror, the stewardess shut the door and the plane began to roll back. Alan Rough was being left behind. I couldn't believe it. Victoria and I stared at each other in total disbelief.

As soon as we touched down in London we called Roughy. It turned out that the airport security had ordered him to go all the way back to the check-in desk with the Skean Dhu. But the desk was closed and by the time he got back to the plane we were already on our way to London, which meant he had to catch the next flight … THREE hours later.

However, in the end the wait was 'worth it'. On his flight down, Roughy was sat next to two lap dancers. What a lucky so-and-so he is!!!

World Cup Questions

5

1 How many World Cups have Scotland qualified for?

(A) 6   (B) 7

(C) 8   (D) 9

2 Who was the top goal scorer at the 1998 World Cup in France?

(A) Zinedine Zidane   (B) Ronaldo

(C) Davor Suker   (D) Rivaldo

3 How many teams competed at the 1930 World Cup in Uruguay?

(A) 11   (B) 13

(C) 15   (D) 17

4 The first-ever World Cup final was played between Uruguay and Argentina. What was the score?

(A) Uruguay 2 Argentina 1

(B) Uruguay 3 Argentina 1

(C) Uruguay 3 Argentina 2

(D) Uruguay 4 Argentina 2

5 At the 1982 World Cup, who scored Scotland's second goal in the 2-2 draw with the USSR?

(A) Alex McLeish   (B) Graeme Souness

(C) Kenny Dalglish   (D) Joe Jordan

6 Who knocked out the Republic of Ireland at Italia 90?

(A) Germany   (B) Holland

(C) Italy   (D) Romania

7 What was the opening game of USA 94?

(A) Germany v USA   (B) Germany v Bolivia

(C) Argentina v USA   (D) Argentina v Mexico

8 At France 98, Scotland drew 1-1 with Norway. Who scored Scotland's goal?

(A) John Collins   (B) Craig Burley

(C) Gordon Durie   (D) David Weir

9 Who did West Germany beat in the 1954 final in Switzerland?

(A) Czechoslovakia   (B) Hungary

(C) Sweden   (D) USSR

10 How many goals in total were scored at the 1962 World Cup?

(A) 79   (B) 89

(C) 99   (D) 109

11 Iraqi defender Barmeer Shaker was given a one-year suspension by FIFA after a 1986 World Cup match. Why?

(A) Punching the referee   (B) Spitting at the referee

(C) Kicking the referee   (D) Kissing the referee

12 At Mexico 86, who scored Scotland's only goal?

13 Who did Scotland play in their opening game of the 1986 World Cup?

14 In which year did the United Arab Emirates qualify for their first World Cup?

(A) 1986   (B) 1990

(C) 1994   (D) 1998

15 Why was the 1974 World Cup final delayed?

(A) One crossbar was broken and needed to be replaced

(B) All the corner flags were missing

(C) The linesman was injured during the warm up

(D) The floodlights failed

16 Who did England beat in the quarter-finals of the 1990 World Cup?

17 Who hosted the 1938 World Cup finals?

18 Who beat France in the opening game of the 2002 World Cup finals?

19 How many players were sent off in total at France 98?

(A) 14   (B) 18

(C) 22   (D) 26

20 Who was in goal for Scotland at the 1986 World Cup in Mexico?

(A) Alan Rough   (B) Jim Leighton

(C) Andy Goram   (D) Bryan Gunn

21 How many World Cup matches were played, in total, between 1930 and 2002?

(A) 544 (B) 644

(C) 744 (D) 844

22 What is the most common score in a World Cup finals match?

(A) 1-0 (B) 1-1

(C) 2-0 (D) 2-1

23 Who was Italy's captain at the 1982 World Cup?

24 In what year did Brazil win their first World Cup?

25 Mexico staged the 1986 World Cup, but which country was the original host of the tournament?

26 Scotland have played 23 matches at the World Cup. How many have they won?

(A) 3 (B) 4

(C) 5 (D) 6

27 Who did Scotland last beat at a World Cup finals?

28 El Salvador have played at two World Cup finals. How many goals, in total, have they conceded?

(A) 18   (B) 22

(C) 26   (D) 28

29 The top goal scorer at the 1974 World Cup was Grzegorz Lato. Which country did he play for?

30 Who was the captain of Brazil at USA 94?

31 Who did Laurent Blanc kiss before every game at France 98?

32 What shirt number did Gary Lineker wear during Italia 90?

33 Between 1930 and 2002, out of these four countries, which has qualified the most times for the World Cup?

(A) Sweden   (B) Holland

(C) Hungary   (D) Poland

34 How many World Cup finals has the Dutch East Indies qualified for?

(A) None   (B) 1

(C) 2   (D) 3

35 Name the three other teams from Scotland's World Cup group at Italia 90.

36 Name Scotland's two goal scorers at Italia 90.

37 Who did Germany beat in the semi-finals to reach the 2002 World Cup final?

38 Name the player who lifted the World Cup trophy at France 98.

39 Who hosted the World Cup in 1962?

(A) Mexico   (B) Chile

(C) Sweden   (D) Italy

40 Italy have won the World Cup four times. In 1934, 1982, and which other year?

(A) 1938   (B) 1950

(C) 1954   (D) 1958

41 West Germany played Holland in the 1974 World Cup final. What was the score?

42 Oleg Salenko of Russia was joint top goal scorer at which World Cup?

43 Who was sent off for Scotland in the game against Morocco at France 98?

44 How many goals have Scotland conceded, in total, at the World Cup?

(A) 37   (B) 41

(C) 45   (D) 49

45 Between 1930 and 2002, which of these four countries failed to score a single goal at the World Cup finals?

(A) Greece   (B) Haiti

(C) El Salvador (D) UAE

46 How many goals did England score at USA 94?

47 At France 98, what was the final score in the group match between the USA and Iran?

48 Who did Sweden beat in the second round at the 1994 World Cup?

(A) Saudi Arabia (B) Bulgaria

(C) Nigeria   (D) Mexico

49 Who scored Scotland's penalty in the 3-2 win over Holland in 1978?

50 Between 1930 and 2002, according to Roughy's calculations, how many fans in total have attended the World Cup finals?

(A) 21 million   (B) 24 million
(C) 27 million   (D) 30 million

To See or Not to See, that is the question

The Sony Radio Awards 2006 were three hours away. I locked the bathroom door of our twin room, as Roughy can't be trusted with his love of practical jokes. I'd only just started wearing contact lenses two days earlier and was having trouble putting them in.

'Come on, Ewen, this is easy,' I said to myself.

The right contact slipped in at the sixth attempt. 'Yussss!' I screamed. Only the left eye to go! I had to get this one first or second time because I was running out of contact solution! First go was disastrous. It nearly dropped to the floor. I should have learned from that because that's exactly what happened next.

'Ohhhhhhhhh ... ya little b******!' I yelped, as it disappeared.

'What did you call me?' shouted Roughy from the bedroom.

'Roughy, I've dropped a contact lens and can't find the blinking thing. Can you come and help me look for it?'

So, there we were, the two of us on all fours feeling around the floor, me stressed beyond belief. I really didn't want to be wearing my glasses to the radio industry's biggest night of the year. However, I didn't have a choice. After 20 minutes of searching, I gave in and put my specs on.

The night itself was fantastic. The biggest names in radio were there along with loads of other celebrities. The disco after the awards ceremony was brilliant and we danced into the wee small hours.

Everything was going fine until a drunken buffoon somehow flicked my glasses off my face and they ended up on the dance floor. I dived to the ground in a way Roughy would have been proud of. But I wasn't quick enough, and my glasses were broken into a million pieces.

Afterwards, we were all standing at the side of the road waiting for a taxi.

'That was brilliant, wasn't it?' said Roughy.

'It's probably one of the best nights I've ever had,' I replied.

'Hey, where's your glasses?' asked Roughy.

'Some idiot stood on them.'

'Oh, that's a shame. If you'd told me earlier I would have given you this.'

Roughy then pulled from his pocket my missing contact lens and burst out laughing.

One day, I will get my revenge!

Scottish Football Mixed Bag

6

1 Who won the Challenge Cup in season 2005/2006?

(A) Hamilton   (B) Clyde

(C) St Mirren   (D) St Johnstone

2 Who lifted the CIS Cup in season 2005/2006?

3 Peter Lovenkrands scored twice for Rangers in their 3-2 victory over Celtic in the 2002 Scottish Cup final. Who scored the other Rangers goal?

(A) Barry Ferguson   (B) Lorenzo Amoruso

(C) Michael Mols   (D) Claudio Caniggia

4 Who finished second behind Gretna in the Second Division in season 2005/2006?

(A) Partick Thistle   (B) Morton

(C) Peterhead   (D) Raith Rovers

5 How many points did Gretna accumulate that same season to gain promotion to the First Division?

(A) 68   (B) 78

(C) 88   (D) 98

6 Which SPL team did St Mirren beat 3-0 in the third round of the Scottish Cup in season 2005/2006?

7 Who won the Third Division championship on goal difference in season 2005/2006?

8 Scotland lifted the Kirin Cup in 2006. Name the two teams they played.

9 Rangers beat Ayr Utd in the League Cup final in 2002. What was the score?

(A) 1-0　　(B) 2-0

(C) 3-0　　(D) 4-0

10 Who missed out on promotion to the SPL in 2003 because they didn't meet the requirements to play in the top flight?

11 Pressley, Skacel, Neilson and who else scored from the spot during Hearts' penalty shoot-out victory over Gretna in the 2006 Scottish Cup final?

(A) Pospisil　　(B) Brellier

(C) Fysass　　(D) Hartley

12 Name the manager who guided Gretna to the 2006 Scottish Cup final.

13 Which club finished bottom of the SPL's Fair Play League for season 2005/2006?

(A) Hearts   (B) Livingston

(C) Falkirk   (D) Hibs

14 Who finished top of the SPL's Fair Play League for season 2005/2006?

(A) Celtic   (B) Kilmarnock

(C) Aberdeen   (D) Inverness

15 Which player finished top of the SPL's 'bad boys league' for season 2005/2006?

(A) Allan Walker of Livingston

(B) Julien Brellier of Hearts

(C) Ivan Sproule of Hibs

(D) Stephen McManus of Celtic

16 Who was Graham Roberts' assistant at Clyde during season 2005/2006?

17 Who finished bottom of the Second Division in season 2005/2006?

18 Who won their play-off final on penalties to reach the First Division in 2006?

19 For season 2005/2006, who had the best home defence in the SPL?

(A) Hearts   (B) Celtic

(C) Rangers   (D) Aberdeen

20 What was the most attended match in season 2005/2006?

(A) Celtic 1 Hearts 1 (the first league game between the two teams)

(B) Celtic 2 Rangers 0 (League Cup victory)

(C) Celtic 1 Hearts 0 (The Hoops win the title)

(D) Celtic 1 Hibs 1 (The day the Hoops are handed the SPL trophy)

21 Name the former Hibs player who guided Cowdenbeath to the Third Division title in 2006.

22 Who replaced John Lambie as manager of Partick Thistle in 2003?

23 Kilmarnock have only ever won the League Championship once. In which year did this happen?

(A) 1962   (B) 1965

(C) 1968   (D) 1971

24 Celtic won the 2005/2006 title with how many games to spare?

(A) Four   (B) Five

(C) Six   (D) Seven

25 How many points did Livingston accumulate in season 2005/2006?

(A) 16   (B) 18

(C) 20   (D) 22

26 Name the manager of St Johnstone during season 2005/2006.

27 Which top-five club did Dunfermline beat 3-0 to reach the semi-finals of the League Cup in November 2005?

28 George Burley only lost one game as Hearts manager. Who was it against?

29 Terry Butcher left Motherwell in 2006 to join which club?

(A) Sydney FC   (B) Melbourne FC

(C) Brisbane Tigers   (D) Adelaide Utd

30 Who replaced Ian McCall as manager of **Dundee Utd**?

31 Who finished behind St Mirren and St Johnstone in the First Division in season 2005/2006?

(A) Clyde   (B) Ross County

(C) Hamilton   (D) Dundee

32 How many points did Rangers get in the 2005/2006 Champions League group stages?

(A) 7   (B) 8

(C) 9   (D) 10

33 Who scored the equaliser for Rangers in the 1-1 draw against Porto in Portugal in November 2005?

34 Who scored Celtic's first goal in their 3-2 win over Hearts on New Year's Day in 2006?

35 Rudi Skacel joined Hearts on loan from which club?

(A) FC Kaunas   (B) Marseille

(C) Sparta Prague   (D) CSKA Moscow

36 East Stirlingshire finished bottom of the Third Division in season 2005/2006. How many games did they win out of 36?

(A) 4   (B) 6

(C) 8   (D) 10

37 Name the two players who scored twice on their debuts for Scotland in the 5-1 victory over Bulgaria in 2006.

38 Who scored the winning goal for Gretna in their 1-0 victory over St Mirren in the 2005/2006 Scottish Cup quarter-finals?

39 Which two clubs won promotion to the First Division in 2004/2005 and were then relegated to the Second Division the following season?

40 Maurice Malpas replaced Terry Butcher as manager of Motherwell. Who did Malpas name as his assistant?

41 Name the Rangers player who was injured while riding his bike in the summer of 2006.

(A) Nacho Novo   (B) Stefan Klos

(C) Marvin Andrews   (D) Thomas Buffel

42 Name the Bordeaux-based Brazilian linked with Celtic during summer 2006.

43 In which Division are East Fife?

44 Who play their home matches at New Douglas Park?

45 What nationality is Hibs midfielder Guillaume Beuzelin?

(A) Italian   (B) Swiss

(C) French   (D) Dutch

46 Celtic defender John Kennedy picked up a serious knee injury playing for Scotland against who?

(A) Poland   (B) Russia

(C) Romania   (D) Hungary

47 Who did Stephen Simmons join after Hearts?

48 How old was Alex Rae when he was appointed manager of Dundee?

(A) 35   (B) 36

(C) 37   (D) 38

49 Who is the owner of Gretna Football Club?

50 Who is the Scottish Football League secretary?

(A) Peter Fonda   (B) Peter Pan

(C) Peter McDonald   (D) Peter Donald

The Return Home

Part 3

07.20

My alarm goes off. 'Oh s***,' I say to myself.

I've only been in bed three hours and I'm a wee bit hung over from our night out at the Sony Radio Academy Awards.

'Get up, Roughy,' I shout. 'We need to get the 8.30 tube.'

'Don't panic, we've got plenty time,' replies Roughy. 'Our flight to Glasgow doesn't leave until 11.35.'

I jump in the shower, get dressed and packed, all in the space of 20 minutes.

'Roughy, I'm off to get some breakfast. I'll meet you down there.'

08.15

Our taxi arrives.

'Notting Hill Gate tube station, mate,' says Roughy.

The taxi takes five minutes. We've got 10 minutes to get to our platform with our luggage in rush hour.

'We need to get on the Central line,' I scream on the escalator.

I march towards the platform, ahead of Roughy and Victoria. Nothing is going to get in my way.

'Ewen, you're going the wrong way,' shouts Roughy.

I stop and look round.

'Trust me, we need to be on the Central line,' I shout back.

By this time I've caused what can only be described as a traffic jam of people.

'Get out the way, you idiot,' snaps a Londoner.

'What did you call me?' I ask angrily.

'You're blocking my way,' he screams.

'Calm down, Ewen, we need to be on the Central line,' says Roughy.

'I bloody know that. Why did you stop me?'

'I just wanted to see what would happen.'

08.40

'Roughy, we've missed the 8.30 train because of your p****** about.'

'Stop your moaning. We'll be there in plenty of time for our flight.'

09.15

We arrive at Liverpool Street Station. We now need to get a train to Stansted. We make our way to the ticket desk.

'Three tickets to Stansted, please,' says Roughy.

'I'm afraid the train can only take you halfway,' says the man behind the glass, 'because of repair work. We've put on buses to take you to the airport.'

'How long will that take?' asks Roughy. 'Because our flight's at 11.35 and we need to check in before 11.'

'The train leaves Platform 2 at 9.30 and will take 30 minutes. The journey on the bus to the airport should take approximately 45 minutes.'

It's going to be tight. We can't afford to have any more delays.

09.58

So far so good. The train leaves on time and arrives a couple of minutes early. But there must be 200 people off this train looking to get the bus to the airport. It is sheer pandemonium.

'Stand against the wall in an orderly queue!' screams a rail employee. As you can imagine, some people don't take too kindly to this, especially those at the back of the queue. Some decide to run to the front.

'Get out of my goddamn way and let me through,' cries an American.

'Sir, if you speak to me like that again you won't be getting on the bus,' replies the harassed rail employee. 'Can you please get to the back of the queue?' He then shuts the gate and refuses to let anyone out until we've 'calmed down'.

Time is against us. I suggest to the man from across the pond: 'Look, mate, we aren't going anywhere fast if you don't get in line and wait your turn like everyone else. Now bug off and shut up.'

10.15

I'm on the bus. However, I've lost Roughy and Victoria in all the confusion. My mobile rings. It's Roughy.

'We're in the bus ahead of you,' says the Scotland legend. 'It's going to be touch and go if we're going to make this flight.'

10.58

Roughy and Victoria are at the check-in desk. I'm five minutes away.

'I'm sorry, sir, the check-in desk is closed,' says the easyJet employee.

'You're having a laugh. We've still got two minutes!' says Roughy.
'I'm sorry, sir, but we've just closed the desk and you won't be getting
on this flight.'

11.15

'Sir, the next flight to Glasgow is at 15.30,' says a pretty girl at the
booking desk.
'We need to be in Glasgow sooner than that,' I explain to Roughy,
'because it's the start of the Real Football Quiz tonight.'
'How about Edinburgh?' Roughy asks the girl.
'Sorry, sir, there's nothing else available.'
We have no option but to take the 15.30 flight to Glasgow. I doubt
we'll get to Real Radio for six o'clock because the M8 between 5 and
7pm is gridlocked. I call the office.
'I don't think we'll make the show on time,' I warn Michael Wilson,
our head of presentation.
'Don't worry about it, we have it all in hand. Just give me a call when
you touch down in Glasgow,' says Michael.

12.30

Roughy, Victoria and I have lunch in an Irish pub.

12.50

Victoria is drunk.

13.30

Roughy and I go and lose some money in the bookies.

15.00

We board the plane to Glasgow. Victoria is a giggling wreck. That's
what cider does.

15.27

The plane takes off early. Woo hoo!

16.25

We land in Glasgow. I kiss the tarmac.

16.30

I call Michael.
'Mate, we've just touched down and we're going to collect our
luggage.'
'Don't worry about your case. Let Roughy and Victoria pick that up. I
want you to run ahead and get here in time for the show.'

'How the hell am I going to do that?'
'"Big D" is waiting for you in the arrivals area. He'll be wearing a leather jacket and leather trousers.'
I have this image of one of the Village People waiting for me.

16.50

I pass through the sliding doors and see mums, dads, brothers, sisters and friends all waiting on loved ones. And there, in amongst them all, is 'Big D'. You can't miss him. Dressed head to toe in black leather.
'Don't shout out my name,' I plead, silently.
'Ewen, over here!' Too late.
'Hey Ewen, I'm here to rescue you. I'll get you to Real Radio in time for your show. My Harley Davidson is outside. The traffic won't be a problem. Let's go!'
Before I can even say hello, 'Big D' grabs my hand and drags me through the airport to his bike. He seems a little excitable and appears to be taking this whole 'rescue' thing very seriously.

17.10

'Big D' throws me a helmet and a pair of gloves ...
'Come on!' he shouts, pounding a clenched fist into the palm of his other hand.
I can't believe I'm getting on a bike with this man. However, I don't have a choice. This is the only way I'll make the show on time. But 'Big D' is brilliant. He dodges in and out of the heavy traffic like a man possessed.

17.50

We arrive at Real Radio with 10 minutes to spare. 'Big D' has done it. He jumps off the bike and gives me a hug. He holds on a little too long for my liking. I escape his clutches and rush into the office to a standing ovation from my colleagues.

The London trip has come to an end ... and I'll never forget it.

Rangers Questions

1 Which former Ger holds the record for most goals scored in a single World Cup match?

(A) Brian Laudrup   (B) Stephane G'uivarch

(C) Oleg Salenko   (D) Nuno Capucho

2 Which Rangers manager gave Derek Ferguson (Barry's older brother) his Rangers debut?

(A) Graeme Souness   (B) John Greig

(C) Walter Smith   (D) Jock Wallace

3 With which club did former Rangers player/manager Graeme Souness start his career?

4 Which former Rangers and Motherwell player also had a stint with Man United?

5 From which club did Rangers sign youngster Danny N'Guessan?

6 Who scored a hat-trick to win the 1983/1984 League Cup final for Rangers?

(A) Ally McCoist   (B) Mark Hateley

(C) Kevin Drinkell   (D) Davie Cooper

7 Who did Rangers secure their first-ever European penalty shoot-out victory against in 2001?

8 Name the 1980s Rangers defender who also plied his trade in England, Northern Ireland and Wales.

9 In his first European match as Rangers manager John Greig scored a victory over which Italian side?

(A) Juventus   (B) Parma

(C) Inter Milan   (D) Napoli

10 In which season did Rangers beat Celtic 5-1 and 4-1 in their home Premier Division fixtures?

11 Which team did Marco Negri score five against in 1997?

12 Who was the first-ever Rangers manager?

13 Which former Rangers manager was known to keep a variety of double-breasted suits in his Ibrox office, often changing two or three times a day?

14 Which three Rangers players, along with Celtic's Frank McAvennie, were charged with 'behaviour likely to cause a breach of the peace' after an Old Firm game in 1987?

15 What career did Davie Cooper have lined up before he signed for Clydebank?

(A) printer   (B) mechanic

(C) builder   (D) joiner

16 In what year did David Murray buy Glasgow Rangers?

17 Which former Rangers player was nicknamed 'The Hammer' by supporters?

18 John Greig holds the record for the most appearances in the Light Blue jersey – but how many did he make?

(A) 655   (B) 755

(C) 855   (D) 955

19 Who was the first Rangers player to bag a hat-trick against Celtic?

20 What was Graeme Souness' first trophy as Rangers manager?

21 From which team did Rangers sign keeper Andy Goram?

22 What was the score when Rangers beat Dynamo Moscow to win the European Cup Winners' Cup in 1972?

23 Who grabbed the goals as Rangers beat Leeds 2-1 at Elland Road in the European Cup in 1992?

24 Rangers became the first Scottish team to reach a European final when they went all the way in the Cup Winners' Cup in 1961. They didn't win but who did they play?

25 Rangers clinched the title on the last day of the 2004/2005 season with a 1-0 win over Hibs at Easter Road while Celtic lost 2-1 to Motherwell. Who scored the Gers goal?

26 In what year did Rangers sign striker Mark Hateley?

27 How many league titles have Rangers won?

28 How many League Cup winners' medals did Davie Cooper win with Rangers?

29 Rangers beat Hearts 5-1 in the Scottish Cup final in 1996. Which Ibrox star bagged a hat-trick?

30 Rangers won the 2002 Scottish Cup final 3-2 against Celtic, but it took a goal in injury time to clinch victory. Who scored it?

31 What nationality is former Ranger Robert Prytz?

32 Stefan Klos won the Champions League with which club before joining Rangers?

33 In 1992 Ally McCoist became the first-ever Scottish player to win the Golden Boot award. How many league goals did he score?

(A) 34   (B) 39
(C) 40   (D) 42

34 Which club did Rangers sell Jonatan Johansson to in 2000?

35 In what year were Rangers formed?

36 Who was Dick Advocaat's first signing as Rangers manager?

37 How much did Rangers pay for striker Tore Andre Flo?

38 Which three players featured in all of Rangers' nine-in-a-row triumphs?

39 In which country was former Ger Terry Butcher born?

(A) England (B) South Africa

(C) Singapore (D) New Zealand

40 What was the name of the Polish defender signed by Dick Advocaat from Dundee in 1999 whose career at Ibrox was hampered by depression?

41 Who scored twice as Rangers beat Motherwell 5-1 to win the League Cup in 2005?

42 At which ground did Rangers clinch nine-in-a-row?

43 Ian Durrant suffered a serious knee injury in 1988, but on which ground?

44 Graeme Souness quit Ibrox five games from the end of which of the nine-in-a-row title triumphs?

(A) first (B) second

(C) third (D) fourth

45 At which stadium did Rangers win the European Cup Winners' Cup?

46 Paul Le Guen will be Rangers manager number....?

(A) 9   (B) 10
(C) 11   (D) 12

47 In what year was Paul Gascoigne named SPFA Player of the Year?

48 How many Scotland caps did Ally McCoist win?

(A) 55   (B) 61
(C) 65   (D) 73

49 Davie Wilson holds the postwar record for most goals in a game by a Rangers player. How many did he score against Falkirk in 1962?

(A) 5   (B) 6
(C) 7   (D) 8

50 For which team did Jim Baxter leave Rangers in 1965?

Ewen: We've passed the halfway stage, big man. What do you think?

Roughy: I'm impressed. Some of the questions were quite difficult.

Ewen: Surely someone with your knowledge and experience in the game would have got more right than wrong.

Roughy: I'm not so sure about that. Why don't you test me?

Ewen: Okay … let me flick through the first chapter. Here we go … You hold a post-war record against England. What is it?'

Roughy: I should get this one. Let me think for a minute.

Ewen: Put the book down, you cheat!

Roughy: I think it has something to do with England. Am I right?

Ewen: Maybe.

Roughy: I think I'm the only goalkeeper to win back-to-back games against England.

Ewen: And?

Roughy: And what?

Ewen: You've missed out one vital piece of information in that answer.

Roughy: I need to go to the toilet.

Ewen: Just answer the question.

Roughy: I can't think properly with a full bladder. I also do my best thinking while I'm in the toilet.

Ewen: Hurry up … and put the book down!

Roughy: I like to have a read while I'm in the toilet.

Ten minutes have passed … and he's not in the toilet.

Ewen: Victoria, have you seen Roughy?

Victoria: He came into the studio five minutes ago and asked me to log onto the inter-net.

Ewen: The cheating git! Did you give him the answer?

Victoria: I couldn't do it because I'm really busy. I think he's in the other studio with Mr. Wilson.

Roughy: I've got the answer! I'm the only Scotland keeper to win back-to-back games against England at Wembley.

Ewen: You got it off the internet, didn't you?

Roughy: Naw.

Ewen: Yes you did. You asked Mr Wilson to look it up for you on the World Wide Web.

Roughy: I haven't got a clue what you're talking about ... we just looked up the answer in his copy of the book!

Ewen: Smart-ass!

Roughy: Ask me another one.

Ewen: Forget it. Coming up next are some interesting pictures.

Roughy: Yes there are! And can I just say that the camera doesn't lie.

Ewen: What do you mean?

Roughy: Well, let's just say you don't take a very good picture. Need I say more?

Ewen: I'm going to slap you. Enjoy the rest of the book.

Here's Roughy and me picking up an award for 'Presentation Team of the Year' at the GMG Radio Awards in 2005. The big boss, John Myers, is on the left and broadcasting legend Mark Goodier is on the right.

We celebrated St Patricks day in grand style. Quite soon after this picture was taken, I was a gibbering wreck. Alcohol and Ewen don't go well together.

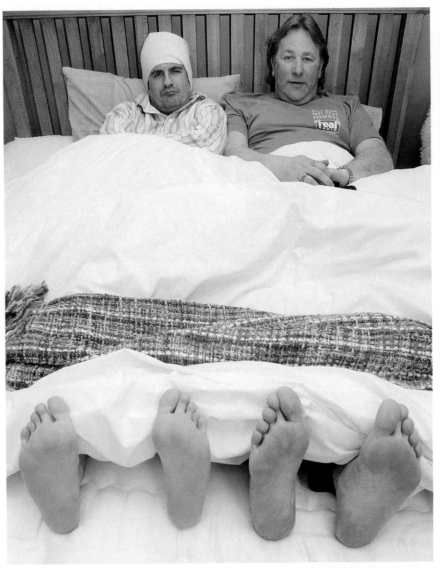

As you will hear on the CD, Roughy and I ended up sharing a double bed the night before the Scottish Cup semi-final between Hibs and Hearts. Our friends at the *Daily Record* decided to re-create that moment.

Real Radio sponsored the Live music stage at 'Big In Falkirk' in 2006. We were mainly interested in Mrs Robinson (above), for obvious reasons, as was boss-man, Jay Crawford on the far right.

Me doing my bit to entertain the thousands at 'Big in Falkirk' 2006.

Here I am getting advice from former top-flight referees, Brian McGinlay and Bobby Tait, before I took charge of the match at Barlinnie. What you can't see is a rather large puddle at my feet!

I may look relaxed....but trust me I've never been so scared in all my life. Unfortunately, the prison guards were not allowed to chaperone me during the game!

One of our listeners decided to mark the anniversary of the last time Hibs won the Scottish Cup by baking Roughy a cake.

Here's Scotland's current number one goalkeeper, Craig Gordon and our former number one promoting Real Radio's Charity Day, 'Bring a Pound to Work'. I think the conversation went something like this: Roughy: 'You'll never be as good as me'. Craig: 'I'd be better than you even if I was blindfolded'.

At the start of season 2005/2006 I was very confident that Falkirk would be relegated. I didn't give them a chance and I gave them a really hard time. A Bairns fan then asked me if I'd put my head in the stocks if Falkirk stayed up. I agreed. It turned out to be a stupid move as you can see. Here is Falkirk manager John Hughes ready to splat me.

Ewen gets the pie.

Alan Rough on tour with Scotland at the World Cup in Spain, 1982.

Roughy on tour with Real Radio, Spain, 2006.

The Good, the Bad and the Ugly, but not necessarily in that order. The good one is Victoria, producer of the Real Radio Football Phone-In.

Here we are again: the occasion this time is the Sony Radio Awards in London. Either side of us is boss-man, Jay (right) and our MD, Billy Anderson. For some reason I am mistaken for the wine-waiter, I can't think why.

Hearts & Hibs Questions

8

1 In which year did Hearts move to Gorgie?

(A) 1874   (B) 1877

(C) 1881   (D) 1883

2 In what year were Hibs founded?

3 In 1896 Hearts beat Hibs in the only Scottish Cup final to be played outside Glasgow. What was the score and where was the final played?

4 Hibs were the first British club to play in Europe. In which year?

(A) 1953   (B) 1954

(C) 1955   (D) 1956

5 Who managed Hearts to Scottish Cup glory in 1956?

(A) Andy Walker   (B) Tommy Walker

(C) Jimmy Walker   (D) Donald Walker

6 Name the Hibs 'Famous Five'.

7 Hearts won the league title in 1958, scoring a record number of league goals. How many?

(A) 128   (B) 130

(C) 132   (D) 134

8 In which year did Hibs first win the First Division title?

(A) 1899   (B) 1903

(C) 1907   (D) 1911

9 In what year was Craig Levein appointed Hearts manager?

10 Who managed Hibs when they beat Real Madrid 2-0 at Easter Road in 1964?

11 Under Craig Levein, Hearts beat Bordeaux 1-0 in the Uefa Cup. Who scored the goal?

12 Who was in goal for Napoli when Hibs beat them 5-0 in 1968?

13 John Robertson was sold to Newcastle in 1988. How much did the English club pay for the striker?

14 In which year did Hearts chairman Wallace Mercer try to take over Hibs?

(A) 1989   (B) 1990

(C) 1991   (D) 1992

15 In which year did Dave McKay make his first-team debut for the Jambos?

(A) 1952   (B) 1953

(C) 1954   (D) 1955

16 Name the European Cup winner signed by Alex McLeish for Hibs in season 1998/1999.

17 Before playing Bayern Munich in the quarter-finals of the Uefa Cup in 1988, Hearts beat St Patrick's Athletic, Austria Vienna and which other club?

18 Who scored a hat-trick for Hibs in their 6-2 win over Hearts in 2000?

19 In February 2000, Hearts fought back from 2-0 down to beat Celtic 3-2 at Parkhead. Who scored the winning goal?

(A) Colin Cameron   (B) Darren Jackson

(C) Gary Wales   (D) Robert Tomaschek

20 Name the Greek side that knocked Hibs out of the Uefa Cup in season 2001/2002.

(A) AEK Athens   (B) Olympiakos

(C) Panathinaikos   (D) Xanthi

21 Including season 2005/2006, how many times have Hearts finished second in the Scottish Premier League?

(A) 1   (B) 2

(C) 3   (D) 4

22 How many goals did Joe Baker score for Hibs?

(A) 129   (B) 139

(C) 149   (D) 159

23 In which year did Hearts play their first game under floodlights at Tynecastle?

(A) 1957   (B) 1959

(C) 1961   (D) 1963

24 How many appearances did Arthur Duncan make for Hibs?

(A) 434   (B) 440

(C) 446   (D) 452

25 What was Tynecastle's capacity between 1954 and 1975?

(A) 39,000   (B) 45,000

(C) 49,000   (D) 53,000

26 Up to and including season 2002/2003, how many times have Hibs qualified for Europe?

(A) 10   (B) 14

(C) 17   (D) 21

27 In what year was Alex MacDonald sacked as Hearts manager?

28 How much did Lokomotiv Moscow pay Hibs for Gary O'Connor?

(A) £1.2m   (B) £1.4m

(C) £1.6m   (D) £1.8m

29 Who did Hearts beat in the 1998 Scottish Cup semi-final?

30 Derek Riordan scored his 50th goal for Hibs in season 2005/2006. Who was it against?

(A) Hearts   (B) Kilmarnock

(C) Aberdeen   (D) Dundee Utd

31 Which two teams did Hearts play in the Uefa Cup group stages at Murrayfield in season 2004/2005?

32 In what year did Pat Stanton leave Hibs for Celtic?

33 In what minute did Stephane Adam score the second goal against Rangers in the 1998 Scottish Cup final?

(A) 52nd   (B) 54th

(C) 56th   (D) 58th

34 Who did Hibs beat in the League Cup final of 1972?

(A) Rangers   (B) Aberdeen

(C) Raith Rovers   (D) Celtic

35 In which year did Gilles Rousset play his first game for Hearts?

(A) 1994   (B) 1995

(C) 1996   (D) 1997

36 How many caps did former Hibs midfielder John Collins win for Scotland?

(A) 38   (B) 48

(C) 58   (D) 68

37 How many penalties did John Robertson score for the Jambos?

(A) 55   (B) 58

(C) 61   (D) 64

38 Hibs won the Scottish Cup for the first time in 1887. Who did they beat?

(A) Queen of the South   (B) Vale of Leven

(C) Third Lanark   (D) Dumbarton

39 During the 1985/1986 season, Hearts went on an unbeaten streak for how many games?

40 Who was manager of Hibs in 1990?

41 In 1896, Hearts beat Blantyre in the Scottish Cup first round. What was the score?

(A) 12-1   (B) 14-1

(C) 16-1   (D) 18-1

42 Hibs hammered Rosenborg over two legs in a Uefa Cup tie in 1974. What was the aggregate score?

(A) 8-3   (B) 10-3

(C) 12-3   (D) 14-3

43 Between April 1989 and April 1994, how many games did the Jambos go unbeaten against Hibs?

(A) 18   (B) 22

(C) 26   (D) 30

44 George Best played less than 20 games for Hibs before he moved to the United States. Name the American soccer team he joined.

45 How many games did Gary MacKay play for Hearts?

(A) 676   (B) 686

(C) 696   (D) 706

46 In which year did Andy Goram leave Hibs?

(A) 1989   (B) 1990

(C) 1991   (D) 1992

47 In season 2005/2006, Hearts signed Mirsad Beslija from which club?

48 Name the Hibs player who was nicknamed 'The Tank'.

49 What shirt number did Roman Bednar wear in season 2005/2006?

50 What nationality is former Hibs player Ulises De la Cruz?

(A) Bolivian   (B) Mexican

(C) Ecuadorian   (D) Peruvian

Every so often Roughy and I will travel with the Scotland squad. It's one of the perks of the job. We've been all over Europe with the national team, hoping to see our boys take a step closer to a major final. However, it's not all work …

The Euro 2004 qualifier, Lithuania v Scotland, was actually the first time we'd taken the show on the road with the national team. You travel with the entire squad and other members of the media. Now, I was a wee bit worried about this, as I didn't have the best of relationships with Berti Vogts. The German should never have been given the Scotland job and I was very vocal in my criticism of him. I was keeping well out of his way.

I was pretty nervous about this flight, not just because of Berti, but also because I'd been very critical of some of the players. However, with it being radio I presumed that most wouldn't recognise me and I'd slip by unnoticed. How wrong I was!

The players and management team boarded the aircraft before anyone else.
'So far so good,' I said to myself.
'Ewen, you've now got to walk past the entire squad at the front of the plane to get to your seat,' said Roughy.
'I'll keep my head down. I'll be ok,' I replied.
'Are you worried?' Roughy asked.
'Naw. I'm fine,' I said. But deep down my stomach was all over the place.

It was now our turn to board the aircraft. Roughy was ahead of me in the queue.
'Hurry up, Roughy! Stop dithering,' I shouted.
'Calm down, you'll be ok,' he said.

It then dawned on me that he was up to no good as a rather large gap appeared between him and the guy in front.
'Roughy, don't you dare do a bloody thing when we get on this plane!' I said.

He ignored me but I could see he was laughing because his shoulders were moving up and down. We stepped onto the plane and there in front of us, in the front row, was Berti Vogts and SFA Chief Executive David Taylor. Behind them were all the players, and that included the under-21 squad.

I put my head down and was focusing on the heels of Roughy's shoes. He was shuffling and then he stopped at the third row of seats. I dared not look up.
'What the hell are you doing?' I wondered inwardly as I continued to stare at the heels of his shoes.
'How are you doing, guys?' said Roughy.
'Oh s***! I'm a dead man,' I said under my breath.
'Are you awright, big man?' said a voice to my left.
'Is that t*** with you?' asked another player.
'It's funny you should ask that. I was about to introduce you to him,' said Roughy.
Roughy turned to me and said 'This is Ewen Cameron.' I wanted the floor to open up and swallow me.
'Yer a f***y, by the way,' said a voice to my right and everyone on the plane burst out laughing.

Let's just say the journey to Lithuania felt like it lasted an eternity. I couldn't wait to get to my hotel room and that in itself is another story. Read all about us watching porn while doing the Football Phone In further on in the book.

1 Name the Scottish goal scorer or scorers when Scotland beat Holland 3-2 in the 1978 World Cup.

2 Name the goal scorer or scorers when Rangers completed nine-in-a-row by beating Dundee United at Tannadice in 1997.

3 Name the goal scorer or scorers when Man United came from behind to beat Bayern Munich 2-1 and win the Champions League in 1999.

4 Who scored the winning goal for Chelsea when they won the Cup Winners' Cup in 1998?

5 Name the goal scorer when Scotland beat England 1-0 at Wembley in 1999.

6 Name the goal scorer or scorers when Hearts beat Bayern Munich at Tynecastle in the Uefa Cup.

7 Who scored the winning goal when Aberdeen won the Cup Winners' Cup in 1983?

8 Name the goal scorer or scorers when Dundee United beat Barcelona 2-0 in the Nou Camp in 1987.

9 Name the goal scorer or scorers when Celtic beat Liverpool 2-0 at Anfield on the way to the Uefa Cup final in 2003.

10 Name the goal scorer or scorers for Celtic when they won the European Cup in 1967.

11 Name the goal scorer when Wimbledon beat Liverpool 1-0 to win the FA Cup in 1988.

12 Name the goal scorer or scorers when Hearts won the Scottish Cup in 1998.

13 Who scored the winning goal when Aberdeen beat Celtic 2-1 to win the Scottish Cup in 1984?

14 Who scored the winning goal when Man United beat Arsenal 2-1 in an FA Cup semi-final replay at Villa Park in 1999? (It was a pretty special goal so you should remember it!)

15 Who scored the goal for France that won Euro 2000 against Italy?

16 Who scored Clyde's second when they beat Celtic 2-1 in the third round of the Scottish Cup in January 2006?

17 Who scored Inverness Caley's third when they beat Celtic 3-1 to go ballistic in the third round of the Scottish Cup back in 2000?

18 Who scored Celtic's fourth when they edged out Juventus 4-3 in the Champions League at Parkhead in 2001?

19 Who scored both Motherwell goals to beat Celtic 2-1 on the final day of the 2004/2005 season?

20 Name the goal scorer or scorers when Liverpool came from behind to beat Arsenal 2-1 in the 2001 FA Cup final.

21 Name the goal scorer when Scotland beat the Netherlands 1-0 at Hampden in 2003.

22 Name the goal scorer when Senegal beat France 1-0 in the opening game of the 2002 World Cup finals.

23 Name the Scottish goal scorer or scorers when Scotland beat Sweden 2-1 at the 1990 World Cup.

24 Name the goal scorer when Scotland beat Switzerland 1-0 at Euro 96.

25 Name the goal scorer or scorers when the Netherlands beat the USSR 2-0 to win Euro 88.

Away in Lithuania — Part 2

We arrived in Lithuania along with the Scotland squad two days before the Euro 2004 qualifier. It meant we had to do the Real Football Phone In from our hotel room on the Monday and Tuesday. The show was coming live from the stadium on the night of the game.

Now, there can be quite a few technical problems hosting a show from a hotel room, and to be honest with you I was slightly worried that we wouldn't be able to do it. As for Roughy, he was more concerned about the night out. He was busily asking our guide about restaurants and nightspots we could visit.

The coach pulled up to our hotel and it looked fantastic. The good news for me was that we had separate rooms. Roughy was on the floor above me. I hurriedly got to my room to see if the ISDN line had been installed and if we'd be able to do the show. The hotel didn't disappoint. Everything was in place and worked perfectly. I could now relax, as there was still three hours before we went on air.

I call Roughy.

'Mate, everything is working fine. I'm going to have a wee sleep. Could you get down here one hour before the show, so that we can get ourselves sorted?'

'Aye, ok. I'm going down to the bar, though, for a couple of beers. I'll see you at five o'clock,' says Roughy.

I go to sleep.

I awake with Roughy knocking on my door. I look at my watch. It's five forty-five.

'Oh s***!' I scream. The show starts in fifteen minutes.

I open the door and Roughy is standing there with a pint of beer.

'Wakey, wakey,' he says.

'What bloody time do you call this?' I demand.

'You said I needed to be here at five and here I am,' he says.

'I meant five o'clock UK time, not local time,' I said in a panicked voice.

'You didn't say that.' And then Roughy burst out laughing.

Luckily for me I'd already set up the equipment before I went to sleep. It was just a matter of calling Real Radio and telling them to dial us in.

We made it … but only just.

The first thirty minutes of the show went well. Technically, everything was sound. I was now relaxing into it and I decided to have a nice can of cold beer from the minibar. Roughy opened up a miniature bottle of champagne and we were having a good laugh with the listeners.

It was now time for a commercial break and also the traffic news. I speak to Chris. He's pushing all the buttons for us in our studio in Glasgow.

'Chris, I need to go to the toilet. How long have I got?' I ask.

'You've got just over three minutes,' says Chris.

'Ok, mate. Roughy, don't touch a thing. I'll be back in a minute.'

As soon as I shut the door to the toilet, I can hear that the TV has been turned on. There's a speaker system in the toilet that is connected to the TV. I can hear that Roughy is flicking through the channels.

It then goes very quiet.

A few seconds later, the TV is back on and all I can hear is a woman screaming that she wants to go 'faster' and that she wants it 'harder'.

I couldn't get out of the toilet quick enough.

Roughy is sat there with the remote control and with a big grin on his face. He'd paid for the porn channel.

*'Ya t****r! That will be billed to my hotel room,' I protest.*

'Don't worry about it. I'll pay for it,' says Roughy.

Chris starts shouting down the headphones.

'You're going live in ten seconds!' he warns.

'Wow! How did she do that? That's mighty impressive! I'll need to try that when I get home,' says Roughy.

'Get that off!' I shout.

He just laughs and puts the remote down the side of his chair. We're back on the air for the second half of the show and there's hardcore pornography on the TV.

'It's the Real Football Phone In ... Live from Lithuania. Have your say on Scotland's must-win game against the Lithuanians on 0845 100 2 101, and before we continue with your calls, Roughy, how do you see this game going?' I ask.

'Very hard, very hard indeed,' he says, his eyes fixed on the TV. 'We need penetration ... and a lot of it. The more penetration we have the better,' he goes on.

At this point I'm gone. I've turned off my microphone and I've buried my face in a pillow.

'We need to get in behind them ... especially down the middle. That's the spot we need to hit,' adds Roughy.

Finding it extremely difficult to speak, I compose myself to ask another question.

'What about the weather conditions ... how will this affect us?'

'I like it better when it's wet … dry isn't good. I hope they spray the surface before the game kicks off,' he says through laughter.

It's at this point I've decided I've got to explain why we're tittering like two little schoolboys.

'The reason we're laughing is because Roughy has just missed his mouth and the champagne is all over his face. Anyway, let's continue with the calls. John in Glasgow, you're on the Real Football Phone In.'

'Hey, Roughy,' says John, 'I heard you prefer to swallow.'

And that was the cue for us to laugh our heads off. That's the head on the top of our shoulders.

1 Who is the world's most expensive player, and how much did he cost?

2 Name the three Dutch internationals who were part of the all-conquering AC Milan side of the late 1980s and early 1990s.

3 After leaving Cruzeiro in his native Brazil, Ronaldo played for three other European teams before his switch to Real Madrid. Name them.

4 Only three clubs have won the European Cup five times or more. Who are they?

5 Which team won the first five European Cups?

6 Which player has won the Champions League with three different teams?

7 From which club did Juventus buy keeper Gianluigi Buffon?

8 How much did Real Madrid pay to land David Beckham from Man United?

9 From which club did Arsenal sign Patrick Vieira?

10 Which three clubs did French great Michel Platini play for during his career?

11 Which club did Rino Gattuso leave Rangers for in 1998?

12 Where did Celtic sign Paolo Di Canio from?

13 Which Italian side did Irish midfielder Liam Brady leave Arsenal for?

14 What is the name of Valencia's stadium?

15 Barcelona won the European Cup in 1992 beating Sampdoria 1-0 at Wembley. Who scored the goal?

(A) Ronald Koeman   (B) Hristo Stoichkov

(C) Albert Ferrer   (D) Pep Guardiola

16 Maradona, Batistuta and Riquelme have all played for them but how many times have Boca Juniors won the Libertadores Cup – South America's equivalent of the Champions League?

(A) 2   (B) 3

(C) 4   (D) 5

17 Which team did Barcelona sign Ronaldinho from?

18 Who was the first English player to win the European Cup with a non-English team?

19 In what year did Paolo Maldini make his AC Milan debut?

20 Romario is one of the greatest goal scorers of all time, and is still scoring today – but which Dutch club did he join when he first left Brazil?

21 How old was Maradona when he made his international debut?

22 With which Norwegian side did former Rangers striker Tore Andre Flo start his professional career?

(A) Sogndal   (B) Valerenga

(C) Brann   (D) Viking

23 Alfredo di Stefano represented three different countries – which ones?

24 With which Portuguese team did winger Luis Figo begin his career before moving to Spain?

(A) Benfica   (B) Sporting Lisbon

(C) Porto   (D) Braga

25 Which Premiership team did Paulo Futre briefly play for during the mid-1990s?

26 Which German outfit did Kevin Keegan join from Liverpool in 1977?

27 What was the name of the keeper who won a staggering 143 caps for Sweden, played in the semi-finals of Euro 1992, and helped Sweden finish third at the 1994 World Cup?

28 Which former German international is the youngest-ever coach to lead a side to the Bundesliga title?

(A) Jurgen Klinsmann

(B) Matthias Sammer

(C) Lothar Matthaus

(D) Karl-Heinz Rummenigge

29 Which Italian striker was nicknamed the 'White Feather'?

30 Which South American star was famous for his oversized crop of curly ginger hair?

31 What was the name of the Russian keeper nicknamed 'The Black Panther'?

32 Brazilian legend Socrates was a wizard with the ball and excelled in which other field?

(A) medicine   (B) veterinary science

(C) law   (D) physiotherapy

33 From which Italian side did Arsenal buy Dennis Bergkamp in 1995?

34 Juventus adopted their famous black and white striped shirt from which English club?

35 Sir Bobby Robson knocked back Hearts but has managed throughout Europe. How many different countries has he coached in?

36 Which player famously had a pig's head thrown at him by Barca fans after switching to Real Madrid?

37 Which team did AC Milan sign striker Andriy Shevchenko from?

38 How many times have Barcelona won the European Cup?

(A) 1   (B) 2

(C) 3   (D) 4

39 Who did Rangers beat to win the European Cup Winners' Cup in 1972?

40 Which country is former AC Milan striker George Weah from?

41 There was an 11-goal thriller in the Champions League in 2003. Dado Prso scored four goals for winners Monaco against who?

42 Toto Schillaci was the surprise top goal scorer at Italia 90, but which Serie A side was he playing for at the time?

(A) Juventus   (B) Fiorentina

(C) Parma   (D) Roma

43 With which team did Eusebio make his name in Portugal?

44 Which club plays at the Stadio delle Alpi?

45 Which two keepers were chosen in the Uefa all-star squad following their performances at Euro 2004?

46 Michael Ballack has won the German title with which two teams?

47 Which member of France's 1998 World Cup-winning squad then scooped £17,000 on a slot machine?

48 Who was the manager of France who famously blamed his side's failure to qualify for USA 94 on David Ginola?

49 Jimmy Greaves had a brief spell abroad with which foreign club?

50 Which team won a hat-trick of European Cups from 1971–73?

The bosses at Real Radio Scotland decided to take the entire station to Torremolinos for the weekend. Roughy and I, Victoria and Stevie McKenna decided to stay at a hotel near Glasgow Airport because our flight to Malaga was at six o'clock in the morning. It meant we had to be at the check-in desk no later than four-thirty. That day we all made the decision to get something to eat and be tucked up in bed before eleven o'clock … Aye right!

Anyway, I had been given the task of sorting out the rooms two days earlier.

Victoria and I go straight to the hotel after the show. Roughy has gone home to get his luggage. Stevie is on air doing the Jukebox and won't be finished until midnight.

'Hello, sir,' says the guy behind the reception desk. 'How can I help you?'
'I have a booking under the name of Cameron,' I say.
'Yes, Mr Cameron, you've booked a family room. How many will be staying?' he asks.
'Just myself and my sister, Victoria,' I reply.
I can see Victoria looking puzzled.
'What the hell is going on?' she asks, as we make our way to the room.
'Look, it's cheaper this way,' I say. 'I don't see the point in us all spending a load of money on four rooms for a couple of hours, so I thought it would be a good idea to get us all into a family room. Roughy and Stevie won't mind. There will be plenty of space,' I say.

How wrong I was! It wasn't the best of rooms.
'Roughy and Stevie are going to slap you!' says Victoria through laughter.
What greeted us was a small double bed and … bunk beds that looked like they'd been made for a ten-year-old.
'Look, I'll just go and book another couple of rooms,' I say.
I pick up the phone.
'Can I book two more rooms, please, for my friends who will be arriving later this evening?'
'I'm sorry, sir, we're fully booked,' says the receptionist.
*The look on my face must have been a picture because Victoria fell onto the bed and nearly p***ed herself laughing.*
'I'm sure the boys will see the funny side when they get here,' I say in hope.

An hour or so later, Roughy meets us in the hotel bar.
'Whose name is my room under?' he asks.
'I've arranged it,' I assure him as I go into my pocket and pull out the key to the family room.
'Right, I'll go and dump my stuff and I'll be back in a minute,' says Roughy.
'Let's follow him,' suggests Victoria.

Roughy is a good few metres ahead of us as we sneak down the hallway going towards our room. We can see the big man slowing up as he approaches our door. He slides the key through the lock and we hear a click. He walks in. We sprint down and place our ears up against the door.
It's deadly quiet for about a minute … I get the impression that he's stood there taking in what he can see. And then it hits him.

'Bloody bunk beds for munchkins!' yelps Roughy. 'He's taking the p*ss!' There's a bang as he throws down his luggage.
'Run, Victoria!' I whisper. 'He's coming out!'
But in our panic to get out of the way we stumble and fall over into a heap on the floor just a few feet from the door. We burst out laughing as Roughy steps out and I burst into song.
'We welcome you to Munchkin Land … tra, la, la, la, la …'

Scotland Questions

11

1 Who played in goal for Scotland during the 2002 World Cup qualifiers?

2 France won 2-0 in a friendly at Hampden in 2000. Who scored the goals?

(A) Wiltord and Henry (B) Dugarry and Henry

(C) Pires and Henry (D) Giuly and Henry

3 Who scored the winning goal against Sweden in a World Cup qualifier at Ibrox in November 1996?

(A) Ally McCoist (B) John McGinlay

(C) Kevin Gallacher (D) Darren Jackson

4 Who captained the team that night against Sweden?

5 Who scored twice in the 3-2 win over Cyprus in 1989?

6 Scotland lost 2-1 to the Czech Republic in a Euro 2000 qualifier. Where was the game played?

(A) Hampden (B) Celtic Park

(C) Ibrox (D) Tynecastle

7 When was the last time Scotland beat England at Hampden?

8 Who delivered the cross for Don Hutchison's headed goal against England at Wembley in a European Championship play-off match in 1999?

9 Who scored the goals in the 2-0 victory over Wales in a World Cup qualifier at Anfield in 1977?

10 Scotland have played Argentina three times. When did they last come head to head?

(A) 1988   (B) 1990

(C) 1992   (D) 1994

11 What was Berti Vogts' first game in charge?

(A) Nigeria   (B) South Korea

(C) France   (D) New Zealand

12 Who scored the goal against Moldova in Chisinau in the 2006 World Cup qualifier?

(A) Neil McCann   (B) Kenny Miller

(C) Steven Thompson   (D) Christian Dailly

13 Who did Scotland play in their opening game of Euro 92?

14 Name the other two teams in Scotland's group at Euro 92.

15 Who captained Scotland in the game against England at Euro 96?
(A) Tom Boyd   (B) Colin Hendry
(C) Gary McAllister   (D) John Collins

16 When did Scotland first play Brazil at Hampden Park?
(A) 1958   (B) 1962
(C) 1966   (D) 1968

17 In which year did Scotland first beat Italy?
(A) 1965   (B) 1966
(C) 1967   (D) 1968

18 Scotland lost 4-1 to South Korea in May 2002. Who scored the goal for the Scots?

19 Scotland beat Spain 3-1 at Hampden in a World Cup qualifier in November 1984. Kenny Dalglish got one of the goals. Who scored the other two?

20 In November 2000, Australia beat Scotland at Hampden Park. What was the score?

(A) 1-0   (B) 2-0

(C) 2-1   (D) 3-0

21 How many times have Scotland qualified for the European Championships?

22 Who was the manager of Scotland for the 1992 European Championships qualifiers?

23 Who replaced Jock Stein as manager for the 1986 World Cup finals?

24 Scotland won 1-0 in Israel in a crucial World Cup qualifier in 1981. Who scored the goal?

(A) John Wark   (B) Kenny Dalglish

(C) Steve Archibald   (D) Archie Gemmill

25 In which year did Scotland first play England?

(A) 1872   (B) 1876

(C) 1880   (D) 1884

26 Spain and Wales were in Scotland's 1986 World Cup qualifying group. Name the other team that featured.

27 Scotland have played the Netherlands 16 times. How many games have the Scots won?

28 Berti Vogts was in charge for the first three games of the 2006 World Cup qualifiers. Name the opposition.

29 Walter Smith's first game in charge was against who?

30 In which year did the Rous Cup begin?
(A) 1983   (B) 1984
(C) 1985   (D) 1986

31 Who won the first-ever Rous Cup?
(A) Scotland   (B) England
(C) Brazil   (D) Chile

32 Scotland played two games in the Kirin Cup in 1995. Who did they play against?

(A) Japan and Brazil

(B) Japan and Ecuador

(C) Japan and Uruguay

(D) Japan and Argentina

33 Who did Scotland play in a World Cup play-off in 1961 at the Heysel Stadium in Brussels?

34 Scotland hammered Yugoslavia in a friendly at Hampden Park in 1984. What was the score?

35 Scotland played in the Brazilian Independence Cup in 1972 against Brazil, Czechoslovakia and who else?

(A) Yugoslavia (B) West Germany

(C) Hungary (D) Italy

36 Who captained Scotland against Brazil at the Maracana in Rio in 1972?

(A) Billy Bremner (B) Asa Hartford

(C) Martin Buchan (D) George Graham

37 Who conceded the penalty that led to Scotland's defeat against Norway in a 2006 World Cup qualifier?

38 Scotland's first appearance at a World Cup was in 1954. Who did they play in their opening game?

(A) Portugal   (B) Austria

(C) Poland   (D) Sweden

39 Who came off the bench to score Scotland's fifth goal against New Zealand at the 1982 World Cup?

(A) John Wark   (B) Steve Archibald

(C) Alan Brazil   (D) Allan Evans

40 Scotland won their first-ever British International Championship match 5-0 in 1884. Who did they play?

41 Scotland played England in the last-ever British International Championship match in 1984. What was the score and where was it played?

(A) 1-1 at Wembley

(B) 1-1 at Hampden

(C) 1-0 to Scotland at Hampden

(D) 1-0 to England at Wembley

42 Scotland beat the CIS 3-0 at Euro 92. Who scored the three goals?

43 Who scored the winning goal for Scotland against Bulgaria in Sofia in a Euro 88 qualifier?

44 How many appearances did Jim Leighton make for Scotland?

45 Brian McClair played 30 times for his country. How many goals did he score?

(A) 1   (B) 2

(C) 3   (D) 4

46 In his 77 appearances for the national team, how many yellow cards did Alex McLeish receive?

(A) 1   (B) 5

(C) 8   (D) 10

47 In which year did Paul McStay make his Scotland debut?

(A) 1983   (B) 1984

(C) 1985   (D) 1986

48 In his 54 appearances for Scotland, how many times was Billy Bremner handed the captain's armband?

(A) 35   (B) 39

(C) 43   (D) 47

49 How many of Jock Stein's 68 matches as manager did Scotland win?

(A) 29   (B) 31

(C) 33   (D) 35

50 How many goals did Kenny Dalglish score for Scotland in 102 appearances?

Ewen: We've come to the end of the book. I hope it was what you expected and more.

Roughy: You've done a good job there, mate. Are we going to do a sequel?

Ewen: That's not up to me. The readers will have to make that decision. However, I'd love to do it again. It was a lot of fun.

Roughy: What would we call the sequel?

Ewen: How about, Ewen and Roughy's Real Football Quiz Book 2?

Roughy: That's rubbish. I've got one for you. Ewen and Roughy Do It Again?

Ewen: Do what?

Roughy: The book.

Ewen: I'm sorry, but that title could be read in so many ways. Do you get what I mean?

Roughy: Oh....aye....I see what you mean. . .

Ewen: I mean, look what happened when we ended up in the same double bed in Edinburgh. Our listeners thought there was more to it than just a booking problem.

Roughy: Ok. We could call the follow up book....em....Ewen and Roughy: Harder than the Last One?

Ewen: Was it?

Roughy: Trust you to twist it,

Ewen: Once again. Thanks for buying the book and CD.

Answers

1. 17
2. 25
3. Switzerland
4. 53
5. 1971
6. 1978, 1982 and 1986
7. Orlando Lions
8. 6
9. Celtic
10. 1981
11. 38
12. England
13. 16
14. Billy McNeill
15. Andy Goram
16. False
17. 2
18. John Blackley and Tommy Craig
19. Davie McParland
20. Kenny Dalglish
21. Jim Leighton
22. 2-0 to Brazil
23. Ally MacLeod
24. Terry Butcher
25. He is the only Scotland keeper to win back-to-back games against England at Wembley

1. Andy Davis

2. 7 – Jim Leishman, Marcio Maximo, Davie Hay, Allan Preston, Richard Gough, Paul Lambert, John Robertson

3. John Robertson

4. Tom Hendrie

5. 2002

6. Celtic, 2003/2004 – 105

7. Jamie McCluskey (aged 16 years, 2 months and 18 days for Hibs against Killie in January 2004)

8. Jim Leighton (41 years, 6 months and 28 days for Aberdeen against Dundee)

9. Aberdeen, 1999/2000 – 83

10. 7 – Tommy McLean, Paul Sturrock, Alex Smith, Paul Hegarty, Ian McCall, Gordon Chisholm, Craig Brewster

11. Graham Weir

12. Rangers and Dundee United

13. Ipswich

14. Chris Sutton and Alan Thompson

15. Sammy the Tammy – Dunfermline

16. Celtic beat Dunfermline 8-1, Hibs were 7-0 winners over Livingston

17. 2002

18. Leicester City

19. £7.5m

20. Henrik Larsson

21. Falkirk won the First Division and should have replaced them but Brockville didn't meet SPL criteria.

22. Chris Sutton and John Hartson, £6m

23. £8.5m

24. St Johnstone

25. Livingston 2005/2006 – 18 pts

26. 60,832

27. Eoin Jess (for Aberdeen against Dundee at Dens Park)

28. Kilmarnock

29. Mark Viduka

30. 2000

31. Ivano Bonetti

32. 7

33. Third

34. 20 years

35. One

36. 2002/2003

37. Stephen Pearson

38. 6,000

39. Ross County

40. Wycombe, Norwich, Leicester City

41. Motherwell, Hibernian

42. Sasa Curcic

43. 74

44. Derek Whyte and Gerry Britton

45. Dundee United

46. 158

47. Emerson

48. 11

49. Fernando Ricksen

50. Michael Gray

1. 92,000

2. Rangers

3. 1892

4. Aberdeen

5. Jimmy McGrory

6. Celtic 7 Rangers 1

7. 1965

8. Scottish Cup

9. Tommy Gemmell and Stevie Chalmers

10. Dixie Deans

11. 1974

12. 25

13. Fergus McCann

14. 1994/1995

15. Dutch

16. Henrik Larsson (hat-trick)

17. 53

18. Celtic 3 Liverpool 1. Celtic 3 Blackburn 0

19. 397

20. £6m for Chris Sutton and John Hartson

21. £650,000

22. Jim Farry

23. Pat Bonner

24. Celtic 11 Dundee 0 in 1895

25. Mark Burchill against Jeunesse Esch of Luxembourg

26. 103

27. 62

28. Brighton

29. Gary Caldwell and Kenny Miller

30. Stevie Chalmers

31. Billy McNeill

32. 37

33. 2000

34. Birmingham

35. Dixie Deans (both hat-tricks were scored against Hibs in 1971 and 1976)

36. Charlie Nicholas SPFA Player of the Year. Paul McStay SPFA Young Player of the Year.

37. 1975

38. £440,000

39. 55

40. 30

41. Dunfermline Athletic

42. West Ham United, Wimbledon and Coventry

43. Dundee Utd (in the Scottish Cup final)

44. 77

45. Boavista

46. Kenny Dalglish

47. European Cup, Scottish League, Scottish Cup, Scottish League Cup and the Glasgow Cup

48. Feyenoord

49. 1957

50. Jimmy Johnstone

The Premiership

1. Brian Deane – for Sheffield United against Man United, 15th August 1992

2. Les Ferdinand – for Spurs against Fulham, 15th December 2001

3. 8

4. 10

5. Andy Cole (Newcastle United) and Alan Shearer (Blackburn Rovers)

6. 34 goals (in 42 games)

7. Dean Richards, Carl Cort, Kevin Davies and Dean Ashton

8. 49 games

9. Man United

10. Grampus Eight

11. Sheffield Wednesday

12. Roy Hodgson

13. £48m (£30m Leeds to Man Utd, £18m West Ham to Leeds)

14. Wimbledon

15. Gordon Strachan

16. 15 – Sunderland, 2005/2006

17. Chelsea

18. Eric Cantona

19. 111

20. Former Pompey keeper Kostas Chalkias (at 1m 99cm)

21. Aaron Lennon (16 years, 129 days for Leeds against Spurs in August 2003)

22. Robbie Fowler (for Liverpool against Arsenal in August 1994)

23. Chelsea, 2004/2005

24. 15

25. Man United, 1999/2000 – 97 goals

26. 21 (Sunderland, 2002/2003)

27. 25 (Chelsea, 2004/2005)

28. Gael Clichy (18 years, 294 days with Arsenal in 2003/2004)

29. Theo Walcott

30. Attilio Lombardo

31. 31

32. Monaco

33. 49/50

34. Gary Speed (and he's still going!)

35. Arsenal

36. One – Davor Suker, Arsenal and West Ham

37. 5:
Arsenal – Cup Winners' Cup 1994
Chelsea – Cup Winners' Cup 1998
Man United – Champions League 1999
Liverpool – Uefa Cup 2001, Champions League 2005

38. Robbie Fowler and Stan Collymore

39. Andy Cole

40. John Terry

41. 4 – Man United, Arsenal, Blackburn and Chelsea

42. Nottingham Forest

43. Celtic

44. Preston North End

45. Paolo Di Canio

46. 11

47. Mimicked snorting coke along the touchline

48. 5 – Sheffield Wednesday, Aston Villa, Bradford, Derby, Middlesbrough

49. 'Tinkerman'

50. Steve Bruce

5

1. 8
2. Davor Suker
3. 13
4. Uruguay 4 Argentina 2
5. Graeme Souness
6. Italy
7. Germany v Bolivia
8. Craig Burley
9. Hungary
10. 89
11. Spitting at the referee
12. Gordon Strachan
13. Denmark
14. 1990
15. All the corner flags were missing
16. Cameroon
17. France
18. Senegal
19. 22
20. Jim Leighton
21. 644

22. 1-0
23. Dino Zoff
24. 1958
25. Colombia
26. 4
27. Sweden (1990)
28. 22
29. Poland
30. Dunga
31. Fabien Barthez
32. 10
33. Sweden (10 times)
34. 1
35. Sweden, Costa Rica and Brazil
36. Stuart McCall and Mo Johnston
37. South Korea
38. Didier Deschamps
39. Chile
40. 1938
41. West Germany 2 Holland 1

42. USA 94 with six goals

43. Craig Burley

44. 41

45. Greece

46. None, because they didn't qualify

47. Iran 2 USA 1

48. Saudi Arabia

49. Archie Gemmill

50. 27 million

Scottish Football Mixed Bag

6

1. St Mirren
2. Celtic
3. Barry Ferguson
4. Morton
5. 88
6. Motherwell
7. Cowdenbeath
8. Bulgaria and Japan
9. 4-0
10. Falkirk
11. Pospisil
12. Rowan Alexander
13. Livingston
14. Celtic
15. Julien Brellier of Hearts
16. Joe Miller
17. Dumbarton
18. Partick Thistle
19. Hearts
20. Celtic 1 Hearts 1 (the first league game between the two teams)

21. Mixu Paatelainen
22. Gerry Collins
23. 1965
24. Six
25. 18
26. Owen Coyle
27. Hibs
28. Livingston in the League Cup
29. Sydney FC
30. Gordon Chisholm
31. Hamilton
32. 7
33. Ross McCormack
34. Stephen Pearson
35. Marseille
36. 6
37. Chris Burke and Kris Boyd
38. Kenny Deuchar
39. Brechin and Stranraer
40. Paul Hegarty

41. Stefan Klos

42. Denilson

43. Third

44. Hamilton

45. French

46. Romania

47. Dunfermline

48. 36

49. Brooks Mileson

50. Peter Donald

7

1. Oleg Salenko

2. John Greig

3. Spurs

4. Andy Goram

5. Auxerre

6. Ally McCoist

7. PSG

8. John McClelland

9. Juventus

10. 1988/1989

11. Dundee United

12. William Wilton

13. Bill Struth

14. Terry Butcher, Chris Woods and Graham Roberts

15. printer

16. 1988

17. Jorg Albertz

18. 755

19. John Barker

20. 1986 League Cup

21. Hibernian

22. Rangers 3 Dynamo Moscow 2

23. Mark Hateley and Ally McCoist

24. Fiorentina

25. Nacho Novo

26. 1990

27. 51

28. 7

29. Gordon Durie

30. Peter Lovenkrands

31. Swedish

32. Borussia Dortmund

33. 34

34. Charlton Athletic

35. 1872

36. Arthur Numan

37. £12.5m

38. Ally McCoist, Richard Gough and Ian Ferguson

39. Singapore

40. Darius Adamczuk

41. Sotirios Kyrgiakos

42. Tannadice

43. Pittodrie

44. third

45. Nou Camp

46. 12

47. 1996

48. 61

49. 6

50. Sunderland

1. 1881

2. 1875

3. Hearts 3 Hibs 1,
   Logie Green

4. 1955

5. Tommy Walker

6. Gordon Smith, Bobby
   Johnstone, Lawrie Reilly,
   Eddie Turnbull and
   Willie Ormond

7. 132

8. 1903

9. 2000

10. Jock Stein

11. Mark de Vries

12. Dino Zoff

13. £750,000

14. 1990

15. 1953

16. Franck Sauzee

17. Velez Mostar

18. Mixu Paatelainen

19. Colin Cameron

20. AEK Athens

21. 4

22. 159

23. 1957

24. 446

25. 49,000

26. 17

27. 1990

28. £1.6m

29. Falkirk

30. Kilmarnock

31. Schalke 04 and
    Ferencvaros

32. 1976

33. 52nd

34. Celtic

35. 1995

36. 58

37. 61

38. Dumbarton

39. 31

40. Alex Miller

41. 12-1
42. 12-3
43. 22
44. San Jose Earthquake
45. 696

46. 1991
47. Racing Genk
48. Eduardo Hurtado
49. 12
50. Ecuadorian

Name the Goal Scorer or Scorers

9

1. Archie Gemmill (2) and Kenny Dalglish

2. Brian Laudrup

3. Ole Gunnar Solskjaer and Teddy Sheringham

4. Gianfranco Zola

5. Don Hutchison

6. Iain Ferguson

7. John Hewitt

8. Iain Ferguson and John Clark

9. John Hartson and Alan Thompson

10. Tommy Gemmell and Stevie Chalmers

11. Lawrie Sanchez

12. Colin Cameron and Stephane Adam

13. Mark McGhee

14. Ryan Giggs

15. David Trezeguet

16. Eddie Malone

17. Paul Sheerin

18. Chris Sutton

19. Scott McDonald

20. Michael Owen

21. James McFadden

22. Pape Bouba Diop

23. Stuart McCall and Mo Johnston

24. Ally McCoist

25. Ruud Gullit and Marco van Basten

World Football 50

10

1. Zinedine Zidane, £47m
   – Juventus to Real
   Madrid

2. Ruud Gullit, Marco van
   Basten and Frank
   Rijkaard

3. PSV Eindhoven,
   Barcelona and Inter
   Milan

4. Real Madrid, AC Milan
   and Liverpool

5. Real Madrid

6. Clarence Seedorf – Ajax,
   Real Madrid and AC
   Milan

7. Parma

8. £25m

9. AC Milan

10. Nancy, St Etienne and
    Juventus

11. Salernitana

12. AC Milan

13. Juventus

14. Mestalla

15. Ronald Koeman

16. 5

17. PSG

18. Steve McManaman
    (Real Madrid)

19. 1985

20. PSV Eindhoven

21. 15

22. Sogndal

23. Argentina, Colombia
    and Spain

24. Sporting Lisbon

25. West Ham

26. Hamburg

27. Thomas Ravelli

28. Matthias Sammer

29. Fabrizio Ravanelli

30. Carlos Valderrama

31. Lev Yashin

32. medicine

33. Inter Milan

34. Notts County

35. 6 – England, Holland, Portugal, Spain, Canada, Ireland

36. Luis Figo

37. Dynamo Kiev

38. 2

39. Dynamo Moscow

40. Liberia

41. Deportivo La Coruna

42. Juventus

43. Benfica

44. Juventus

45. Antonios Nikopolidis and Petr Cech

46. FC Kaiserslautern and Bayern Munich

47. Emmanuel Petit

48. Gerard Houllier

49. AC Milan

50. Ajax

1. Neil Sullivan	21. Twice (1992 and 1996)
2. Wiltord and Henry	22. Andy Roxburgh
3. John McGinlay	23. Alex Ferguson
4. Colin Hendry	24. Kenny Dalglish
5. Richard Gough	25. 1872
6. Celtic Park	26. Iceland
7. 1985	27. 6
8. Neil McCann	28. Slovenia, Norway and Moldova
9. Don Masson and Kenny Dalglish	29. Italy
10. 1990	30. 1985
11. France	31. Scotland
12. Steven Thompson	32. Japan and Ecuador
13. Holland	33. Czechoslovakia
14. CIS and Germany	34. 6-1
15. Gary McAllister	35. Yugoslavia
16. 1966	36. Billy Bremner
17. 1965	37. James McFadden
18. Scott Dobie	38. Austria
19. Mo Johnston	39. Steve Archibald
20. 2-0	40. Northern Ireland

41. 1-1 at Hampden

42. Paul McStay, Brian McClair and Gary McAllister

43. Gary MacKay

44. 91

45. 2

46. 1

47. 1983

48. 39

49. 29

50. 30